WILDFLOWERS
OF MOUNT RAINIER AND THE CASCADES

Text: Mary A. Fries

Photos: Bob and Ira Spring

Special acknowledgement to Patricia Spring
(Ira's wife) who lent a woman's patience and
fortitude and took about half of the photographs in this book.

THE MOUNT RAINIER NATURAL HISTORY ASSOCIATION
AND THE MOUNTAINEERS

1

THE MOUNTAINEERS

Organized 1906

To explore and study the mountains, forests, and watercourses of the Northwest;

To gather into permanent form the history and traditions of this region;

To preserve by the encouragement of protective legislation or otherwise the natural beauty of Northwest America;

To make expeditions into these regions in fulfillment of the above purposes;

To encourage a spirit of good fellowship among all lovers of outdoor life.

First Edition, May 1970

Copyright © 1970
The Mountaineers, Seattle, Washington 98111
P.O. Box 122

Manufactured in the United States of America by
Craftsman & Met Press
Seattle, Washington

Book design by Marge Mueller
Library of Congress Catalog Card No. 70-123996

Cover photo: Flower field on the side of Alta Vista; glacier-clad Mount Rainier in the background. Taken in early August on a 4x5 Super Graphic camera with a 127mm Optar lens and Professional Ektachrome film.

INTRODUCTION

This book of color photographs is designed to help visitors get acquainted with wild flowers of the Northwest, particularly those growing in the mountains. The emphasis is on appreciation, on the place of the plant in the flora of the Cascades, and on interesting facts the reader can associate with the flower to help him remember it. The photographs were taken in the Cascades, mainly around Mount Rainier and northward to the Canadian border.

The majority of the flowers are those found in areas of most floral interest to the average person, flowers growing in mountain forests and subalpine parklands. A few flowers more characteristic of lower elevations, but growing some distance up into the mountains, are included. Some alpine plants also are pictured; speaking in the strict, technical sense of the word, "alpine" vegetation in the Cascades is quite limited.

The photographers think it is a book you will want to keep on your coffee table and enjoy at home. Though the text is obviously intended to be read at leisure, the author wishes also to suggest that you pick a good day, take along a watertight wrapping for insurance, but *do* carry the book on a few mountain trips and use the pictures for your first identification attempts.

Trying to go from book to flower is guaranteed to prove frustrating. It will be more rewarding to look at flowers in the mountains, then look through the book for a photograph matching what you saw. Since many of the more conspicuous species are included here, chances are you often will find a picture of the flower seen, or of one so similar that a reading of the text will give either a name or some clues to help you use identification manuals. On the other hand, expect to see many others; only a limited number can be included in a book like this.

Though technical descriptions of our flowers are adequately available, there is as yet not much published ecological information. While we know quite a bit about which plants grow where, we know very little about why. Most of the comments included are based on personal observations by the author and other hillwalkers interested in flowers. To these have been coupled some of the factors now known to be of general importance that appear applicable. These impressionistic generalizations undoubtedly will be refined as more detailed studies are made. In the meantime, do look and see what you can figure out yourself.

The authority for the scientific names is *Vascular Plants of the Pacific Northwest,* by C. Leo Hitchcock, Arthur Cronquist, Marion Ownbey, and J. W. Thompson. A great deal of thought was given to the choice of common names so that people would find them truly usable. They come from various published sources and were chosen by applying criteria of appeal, ease of use, and adequate distinctiveness. At this time many mountain plants cannot be said to have truly common names; people need more acquaintance with these flowers before their names can become part of our language. For this reason frequent comments on names have been made in this book.

It is conventional to italicize or otherwise distinguish scientific names; the genus or first part of the binomial is always capitalized. When suggested by the author as a common name, as we all use aster, phlox, rhododendron, and others, this generic name has not been capitalized or otherwise distinguished from the rest of the text. Readers are not limited to our suggestions; in the absence of other good words, people may make common names of any genus they desire (but not from the specific or second names alone, which are meaningless by themselves). In matching up information from various sources, however, the complete scientific name should be used—that is its purpose.

Sizes are mentioned as rough generalizations to give the reader some idea of what is represented by the photograph; actual sizes in the field may vary considerably. Places where particular flowers have been seen by the photographers or author are suggestive only, by no means exhaustive. When available, the time of year when the photograph was made is included for its interest. However, depending upon elevation, winter snow depth, whether a cool or sunny site, and other factors, the same flower may be seen earlier or later.

Little clues found by the author to be identification helps might well be jotted in a portable notebook as a reminder to notice these details when you find a flower whose photograph you want to check when you get home. Technical words used for preciseness, and a few picturesque ones whose meaning may not be clear to all readers from the context, are explained briefly by catchword or phrase. For fuller definitions refer to such sources as the excellent illustrated glossaries found in plant manuals.

The author wishes to thank the many people who over the years have answered her questions; and also, those people who have asked her for information, thereby inspiring further study, as well as, unaware to both sides, building a fund of material known to be of interest to the typical wildland traveler. Information has been gleaned from too many books and periodicals to list. For special help we wish to express appreciation to these persons in particular:

Elizabeth Carlson and the early "botany bunch" of The Mountaineers, who collected information and passed it on;

Norman Bishop and others of the National Park Service for courtesies and suggestions extended;

V. J. Krajina, University of British Columbia, for permission to adapt material on some of the forest plants from the *Ecology of Western America, Vol. 1;*

Mr. Douglas Henderson, University of Washington, and Dr. Richard W. Fonda, Western Washington State College, for reviewing the manuscript.

HINTS ON FLOWER PHOTOGRAPHY

Photographing wildflowers is easy if you have the right camera, good weather, and the energy to hike a bit. Other helpful traits are: the disposition to fiddle with a tripod, the willpower to ignore mosquitoes, and the patience of Job to wait for a moment of calm between gusts of wind.

Take only pictures, leave only footprints. In Mount Rainier National Park the alpine flower fields are enjoyed by thousands of people annually, but they are very fragile. Whether inside or out of a national park, don't pick the blossoms or the flowers won't reseed. Step on them and the blossoms are broken off. Stay on the trails because a few careless feet can cause erosion gullies. When taking pictures, leave the flowers in place and take care not to trample a hundred while photographing one.

Many of the pictures in this book were taken with a 4x5-inch view camera, but generally the 35mm camera is best for flower photography. Regardless of size, if you want to shoot close-ups, through-the-lens viewing is needed for accurate composition and focusing. Most of the new model 35mm cameras costing $100 or more have this feature. They are referred to as single-lens reflex cameras and cost anywhere from $100 to $1,000. Most are good. The more expensive merely have additional refinements and accessories.

Most 35mm cameras have a 50mm lens (that just means 2 inches long) which focuses from infinity to about 2½ feet. You can buy an inexpensive accessory called a close-up lens that allows focusing to less than 2½ feet. For extreme close-ups of individual blossoms, you must have a camera that will accept extension tubes or extension bellows. These enable you to move in very close and get life-size pictures. Extensions are available for almost any camera that has interchangeable lenses.

Single-lens reflex cameras are available that use 120-size film, and at least one of the instant-loading cameras will work for flower photography. View cameras with their built-in bellows will focus in larger-than-life size. Larger cameras, 4x5-inch to 8x10-inch film size, give beautiful results, but are awkward and heavy, and the film is expensive. Most professionals and amateurs prefer the smaller cameras.

The standard 50mm lens is adequate, but for extreme close-ups, say at 1:1 (life size) a 100 or 200mm lens is easier to use. With a shorter focal length like 50mm, moving the camera an inch closer or farther away from the flower causes a radical change in the size of the flower on the film. Working with a longer focal length, 100 or 200mm, the camera can be farther away from the subject and the image size then changes less radically with fore-aft movements of camera position. This also helps to keep you back out of your own light and is how the picture of the bee on the thistle was taken (page 152). The long focal length lens can also give interesting perspectives of background. In one case, as the long lens narrows the field, you might be able to eliminate trees that intrude on your blue sky, such as the columbine blossom on page 125. On the other hand, you might want to emphasize a distant mountain as we have with Sloan Peak on page 140.

A tripod is essential for the long exposures needed for good depth of field in close-ups. Exposure times will often be up to a half-second. A tripod is also needed for careful focusing and composing on close-ups. For flowers, the camera is often set at ground level, and a tripod should support a camera from one inch to 4 feet above the ground. Most tripods won't adjust to ground level, but on some it is possible to reverse the center post. (Hold onto the camera until all knobs are re-tightened!) When reversed, the tripod holds the camera upside down (be sure it is on tight) and must be manipulated between the legs of the tripod. It's awkward but works.

Flowers spend most of their existence bobbing in the breeze (and in the Northwest, in the rain). To a casual hiker they may look still, but stop and watch a single blossom. Line it up between two sticks and see how much movement there is. Taking close-ups may be impossible on a windy day and difficult enough on what non-photographers consider a calm day. Even the calmest day has small breezes; tall flowers, particularly, are seldom still. Patience is the word, and lots of it. There are momentary lulls. Wait a minute or 10 minutes. Don't give up. Eventually (maybe next Tuesday) the flower will hold steady for a brief moment. Try rigging a piece of clear plastic for a wind-break, or set up a clear plastic umbrella. Shutter speeds of 1/250 second will stop flower movement in anything but a gale. 1/60 second will stop a gentle movement, but for any speed less than 1/25 the flower must be perfectly still. Use a cable release to keep your own motions from moving the camera when taking long exposures.

"Depth of focus" or "depth of field" refer to the ability of the camera lens to make an in-focus image of a flower in the foreground and also to make an acceptably sharp image of the leaves or scenery in the background. Maximum depth of field is obtained by closing the aperture of your lens to its smallest possible opening. On some cameras this is f16, on others f22 or f32. Most cameras have a depth of focus scale. The instruction booklet that comes with your camera will explain its use. You can see the effects of stopping down by manually closing the lens aperture while looking through the viewer. The birdsbeak pedicularis on page 172 is an example of using a short depth of field to put an unwanted or confusing background out of focus. On the other hand, the wild buckwheat on page 200 needed the maximum depth of focus.

Your exposures generally will be a compromise between speed to "stop" movement and a small aperture to get the maximum depth of focus. Use an exposure meter pointed at the flowers as a guide. When you use the bellows or extension tubes to focus on a close subject, the lens is farther from the film and the f numbers are no longer accurate. Therefore, close-ups require a larger aperture for normal exposure than subjects at infinity. You must allow a full stop more for close-ups (or exactly what the meter says, if not a close-up). Take at least three exposures, one at the correct exposure and one each about two-thirds over and two-thirds under. Through-the-lens meters solve several problems associated with close-up light. They give good results but take a greater understanding to adjust so a bright flower with a dark background will be properly exposed. When all else fails, read the instruction book that came with your camera.

For flower fields with blue sky and snow-covered mountains, Kodachrome II gives good results. However, for close-ups, use a fast color film such as High Speed Ekta-chrome, which narrows down the compromise between the aperture opening needed for maximum depth of field and still allows a shutter speed fast enough to "stop" some of the movement of the flower.

Heavy shadows are sometimes a problem when taking flower pictures. A white cardboard or coat can be used to reflect sunlight into the shadows. Some photographers carry a roll of aluminum foil for this purpose. Remember to re-read your light meter after adjusting the amount of light. A light coat was used for a number of photos in this book.

You may want to use artificial light, too. Flashbulbs or electronic flash units can be used close up, but flash-to-subject distance is very critical. The lighting can easily look artificial with the fill-in light stronger than the sunlight. For this reason, none of the photographs in this book were taken with flash.

Blossoms often look best with late-afternoon light such as the mountain daisy on page 144. To make a flower stand out against a black background, carefully shadow the ground, not the flower, with a coat.

Cloudy or rainy days are generally best for shooting flowers in the woods. Examples are the linnaea or twinflower (page 40), oak ferns (pages 16-17), Indian pipe (page 60), and many more. Raindrops make the flowers bob much as wind does in open meadows. A drop hitting a blossom can't be predicted so be prepared to take extra exposures in hopes that at least one time the flowers will be still.

Some extras that will help are knapsack, waterproof pants or small tarp to kneel on while photographing in marshy places, a notebook and pencil to keep track of exposures used, and a good insect repellent. Also, don't forget the tripod, light meter, cable release, wind screen, reflector, close-up lens, extension tube, extra film, and camera.

Most photography textbooks give instructions for taking flower pictures. However, Eastman Kodak's *Here's How* booklets have short and very good instructions. Try: Eastman Kodak's *The Third Here's How* (AE 84), page 22, "Photographing Wildflowers," and *The Fifth Here's How* (AE 87), page 11, "Creative Close-ups of Flowers."

Bob and Ira Spring

THE MOUNTAINEERS: AN INVITATION

The Mountaineers, with groups based in Seattle, Everett, Tacoma, and Olympia (and groups elsewhere in the planning stage) warmly invite the membership of all lovers of outdoor life who sympathize with the purposes of the organization and wish to share its activities.

The Mountaineers sponsor a year-around program of climbing, hiking, camping, ski touring, and snowshoeing. Many hundreds of outings are scheduled each year, ranging from afternoon walks to trips lasting 2 weeks or more. On a typical weekend as many as 50 excursions may be offered, from ocean beaches to the summit of Mount Rainier. In addition, members engage in countless privately-organized trips of all kinds; the opportunity is boundless to make new friends with similar interests.

Enjoying wildlands is one side of the coin; the other is working to preserve the natural beauty of Northwest America. Here, The Mountaineers continue their role of leadership as they have for more than 60 years.

For a membership application, and further information on club activities, write The Mountaineers, P.O. Box 122, Seattle, Washington 98111.

SELECTED REFERENCES

Hitchcock, C. Leo, Arthur Cronquist, Marion Ownbey, and J. W. Thompson. *Vascular Plants of the Pacific Northwest*, University of Washington Press, 1955-1969. A five-volume set covering all plants growing wild in the Northwest except mosses, liverworts, lichens, and fungi. There is an illustration for each, and even a person with limited technical background, if he knows enough about flower families to pick the section in which to start looking, can use the detailed line drawings to narrow the choice, and then study the corresponding keys and full descriptions. The set has a number of other helpful features, such as notes about the garden possibilities when known, lists of synonyms, derivation of scientific names. Available for reference in larger libraries, and flower enthusiasts may wish to own personal copies.

Jones, George N. *The Flowering Plants and Ferns of Mount Rainier,* University of Washington Press, 1938. An identification manual such as this one, which is complete for a small area, provides an intermediate stop if the above set proves to be a giant step beyond the book of color photographs now in hand. Keys are simple, and since many of the plants grow beyond the boundaries of the title, the Jones book is worth carrying in other mountains of Washington. Because it was written during a period when "splitters" were in the ascendancy among botanists, Jones includes some separate names which are not now recognized for our plants. To make it easy to relate these names, they have been mentioned in the present book. It is helpful to mark your personal copy of Jones and the current names and those species which are now "lumped."

An inclusive book covering North Cascades National Park will serve a similar purpose. If even a small technical manual seems too long a step, work up to it by using other popular illustrated books which include flowers of the Cascades. Information and flowers included by each author vary, and something can be learned from each.

Gunther, Erna. *Ethnobotany of Western Washington,* University of Washington Press, 1945. Lists information obtained by interview, on the Indian uses of plants for food, medicine, and other purposes before the white man came. No illustrations, but scientific names can lead you to illustrations in other books.

Craighead, John J., Frank C. Craighead, Jr., and Ray J. Davis. *A Field Guide to Rocky Mountain Wildflowers,* Houghton Mifflin Company, 1963. While not of use as an identification guide in the Cascades, people interested in edible plants will find for species we share with the Rockies, some interesting notes on their use as food, as forage, or on poisonous properties.

Wild Edible and Poisonous Plants of Alaska, University of Alaska Cooperative Extension Service, Pub. No. 40, rev. 1966. Includes their preparation also. Again, it is necessary to pick out the species we share with them. Checking has to be done by the scientific name, because of the variability of common names. Both this and the Craighead book are illustrated with color photographs and line drawings.

Taylor, T. M. C. *The Ferns and Fern-allies of British Columbia,* British Columbia Provincial Museum, 1956. Close enough to include most of our ferns, and a convenient separate for those especially interested in these plants. Detailed line drawings of each species. Same institution has a series of booklets, including common mosses, mushrooms, and other groups.

Brooks, Maurice. *The Life of the Mountains,* McGraw-Hill Book Company, 1967. An introductory overview of mountain ecology, including ranges all across the continent.

Skunk cabbage (Lysichitum americanum)

Residents of Western Washington know they are "east of the mountains" when they see the ponderosa pine. This is the lowest of the forests on the eastern slopes of the Cascade Range. The climate is arid enough for moisture levels to be much more critical on the east side than on the west, and apparently foresters expect to recognize a number of zonal levels. The rest of us are aware of a great mixture of species growing just above the ponderosa pine, in a forest that is not as tall and not as shady as the best-developed ones on the west side. While among the ponderosa pines most of the conspicuous flowers are quite different from anything we know on the rainy side of the mountains, the next forests have many flowers in common with the west. Engelmann spruce, its needles sharp-tipped, and joining in a little higher, the subalpine fir, indicate that we are getting into the high country.

On the abstract range we form in our minds (rather like a long shed with no sidewalls but with roofline extending to the base on both sides), the western slope is quite different. Not only is the forest more dense, but its tree components have changed in relative importance. The highest forest, in part open, contains mainly mountain hemlock, subalpine fir and Pacific silver fir. Generally, the subalpine fir is slated to be replaced by one or both of the others, it is now thought. Farther down, on our way back home, we notice that Pacific silver fir is the dominant tree. It forms quite a thick forest,

we rarely are aware of the sky, but we see many small saplings growing up in this shade. They have flat branches, with several rows of needles lying on top, pointed toward the outer tips. Still lower the western hemlock, its small cones scattered all over the trail, appears to be the most common tree. At its own best level, it is also considered to be a dominant. There are often many trees of various ages, quickly recognized even from a distance by the drooping leader. Douglas fir does not match up exactly with one of these west-side zones, but is usually the result of a past history of fire.

Trees, when present, dominate both the landscape and other plant life growing with them. Therefore a better understanding of the flowers comes from noticing whether trees, and which ones, are associated with the flowers at which we look. A few broad terms are helpful to sort out the many impressions we gain from even a single trip to the mountains. Beginning from the bottom: lowland forest, then the montane forest at middle altitudes, and finally the subalpine forest. At upper, unforested levels are the subalpine parklands with some trees, and higher yet, alpine vegetation. Zonal differences are an expression of the effective length of the growing season. Along with altitudes, attention should also be paid to habitats, how wet to dry, how cool to warm; and to communities, plants that seem to be associated with each other.

Skunk Cabbage   *Lysichitum americanum* (Arum Family)

One of the earliest signs of spring is the skunk cabbage. The bright yellow spathes (hoods) enclose a thick club-like flower stalk with closely-set small green flowers. These develop first, and large green leaves, which give the plant the name of cabbage, come later. Both are odorous, which explains the rest of the name. Actually not very mephitic, the fragrance of the flowers is at first very sweet, almost overpowering, apparently serving to attract small flies and other dipterous insects which act as pollinating agents. Wilting flowers, broken stems, and crushed leaves have more of a skunk smell.

This northwesterner is abundant in wet swampy hollows where water remains close to the surface throughout the season. As in the photograph, it is frequently associated with red alder. Also with western red cedar, and at its highest levels it may consort with the lowest-level marsh marigolds. Like its eastern relative, the purplish-flowered *Symplocarpus foetidus,* the yellow skunk cabbage forms a thick, dominant blanket of green ground-cover through which no other plant can grow. A white-flowered species, more closely related to our yellow one, grows in Japan and northeastern Asia. Skunk cabbages belong to the arum family along with calla lilies and anthurium. The name "lysichitum" means a loose tunic or mantle, referring to the spathe.

Despite their hot peppery quality, skunk cabbage leaves are apparently relished by mountain beaver, burrowing rodents not closely related to beaver but similar in their habits of nipping off limbs from bushes or young trees and being active at dusk or in the night; they are also haymakers like the pika. Deer also eat the leaves. Bears dig out the fleshy rootstocks, which are peppery, too.

Photographed in mid-May, with a 4x5-inch camera, near Silverton on the Mountain Loop Highway. The tripod had to be set up in the mud.

11

Trillium (Trillium ovatum)

Trillium (Trillium ovatum), double form

Trillium (Trillium ovatum)

Trillium

Trillium ovatum (Lily Family)

The trillium is another flower intimately associated with spring, but later than the skunk cabbage. Now spring is really here. Trillium blooms by the calendar; whether the weather has been warm or cold does not make much difference — growth, as with most plants, is triggered by increasing length of days. In the mountains, however, the winter snow blanket prevents growth from starting until it has mostly melted, so one can follow spring up the mountainside and find trilliums blooming in newly-uncovered ground. In contrast to the skunk cabbage whose buds come out of the ground point first, trillium emerges bottoms up, leaves curled around the flower bud, and turns over as it develops.

Occasionally, double forms of trillium are found. Avalanche lilies have been recorded with 4, 8, and 21 petals; double western anemones have also been seen. Often the extra petals represent missing parts, such as stamens, so plants of this type do not reproduce themselves, unless helped by man to multiply vegetatively, which is the way we maintain many of the double forms of plants in our gardens. For this reason, these mutations are not as often seen in the wild as some other kinds, such as albino plants, which do have some chance of perpetuating their kind.

(Top) Photographed on a rainy day, alongside the Boulder Creek trail in the Suiattle River valley, with a 4x5-inch camera.

(Bottom) Double trillium near Verlot, photographed in early June with 4x5-inch Super Graphic.

Color mutations affect blue, purple, and pink flowers particularly. White-flowered forms of bleeding heart, shooting star, dwarf fireweed, kalmia, red heather, and pink monkeyflower have been seen among the common pink ones. Typically blue lupine, larkspur, and veronica have been seen in the Cascades in both pink and white.

This Northwest lowlander climbs surprisingly high into the mountains, where it may be seen blooming as much as 3 months later than on Puget Sound. Near sealevel trillium is associated with Easter and spring vacation; up in the mountains it has to wait until the snow melts.

Yellow stamens set off the petals, which are pure white at first, fading to a pinkish-purple color with age. As is typical with members of the lily family to which it belongs, flower parts come in threes. In this case three green sepals are much smaller than the petals, thereby differing from some of the other lilies, such as the avalanche lily which has six parts looking alike. Trillium also has three leaves, arranged in a whorl just below the flower, and developing at the same time. It is impossible to pick a trillium without taking all three leaves, thereby leaving the rootstock with no means of renewing its reserves for next year's growth. New leaves will not grow until next season, and it may take some years before the plant is again able to bloom.

Trillium ovatum grows from British Columbia to Montana and southward through Washington, Oregon, and the Coast Ranges of California. It was first collected by Meriwether Lewis in April 1806, below The Dalles on the Columbia River, as his party returned east. In favorable situations quite large colonies will be formed in woods at low elevations.

Trillium turning purple with age, photographed in mid-July at the 4000-foot level on the side of Rock Mountain near Lake Wenatchee. On High Speed Ektachrome with a 35mm Canon. For a notable display of this flower in the lowlands visit Penrose State Park in May.

Oak Fern *Gymnocarpium dryopteris* (Fern Family)

The fern pattern here includes no flowers, ferns belonging to a group of plants which reproduce by means of spores instead of flowers and seeds. A similar site in shaded forest could as well have a pattern composed of leaves of various shapes—of several kinds of ferns plus shade-tolerant flowers. These oak ferns emphasize the triangular, repeating this form twice in each delicate lacy frond sent up at random from slender, creeping underground stems. Placed horizontally on a 6-inch stipe (stalk), the leaves are ideally positioned to provide their best view when seen from above as one walks along the trail. Oak fern may also be spotted in the following picture of the foamflower (p. 24), and with the devil's club photograph as well (p. 21).

Oak fern is found in cool, moist forests, in our area usually in the mountains, in situations where there is permanent underground seepage from slopes above, or on stream terraces where the water table is fairly high. In the past often listed as *Dryopteris linnaeana,* it ranges across the northern part of North America and to Eurasia.

Some kinds of ferns have adapted to full sunshine, as the parsley fern and the lace fern; some, like the licorice fern which grows on mossy rocks or maple limbs, can take quite long dry periods. Regardless of the conditions which can be endured by the mature plant, ferns can grow only in places where the gametophyte stage finds enough moisture at the right time. More often met in the moist conditions associated with forests, it is these environmental requirements for the production and establishment of the young plant that determine where ferns are found. The spore, produced by the plants we know as ferns, in turn grows a tiny, inconspicuous body called a prothallium. For its growth moisture needs to be close to the surface. This generation is bisexual and requires a bit of water also, to unite sperm and egg and start a new fern. And so, we associate ferns with shady places.

Oak ferns photographed with a 4x5-inch camera during a rainstorm, on the Ohanapecosh River trail, one of the best places to see this fern in Mount Rainier National Park. Equally good displays can be seen on the Thunder Creek trail near Diablo.

Ferns

Leaf patterns formed by ferns are as many as the kinds of ferns. Big clumps of sword ferns under a patch of alder remain green all winter, fronds radiating from a short, thick rhizome (underground stem). They are also found in the Douglas fir forest, where their presence indicates good timber growth associated with stored moisture in deep fine-textured soils or seepage moisture below ground bringing both water and nutrients from higher slopes. The sword fern (*Polystichium munitum*) is related to the Christmas fern, and picked in certain areas for use by florists. (See the devil's club photograph for a picture of it.) Deer fern (*Blechnum spicant*), associated especially with western hemlock, is a smaller evergreen, with a circle of one type of tough leathery leaves lying on the ground, and another type growing upright in its center during early summer, bearing the spores. Much-divided lacy fronds of lady fern (*Athyrium filix-femina*) grow 3 feet tall in more moist conditions, such as a streambank or swamp. Maidenhair fern (*Adiantum pedatum*), with delicate leaflets arranged palmately like the fingers of a hand on long black, wiry stalks, is apt to be seen decorating a shady ravine where it is almost constantly sprinkled by water. Maidenhair and lady ferns both die back in winter.

On sunny, crumbling cliffs where it may dry out, but that does not seem to hurt it, is found a small lace fern (*Cheilanthes gracillima*), making do with a minimum of soil, tiny oval leaflets incurled and hairy to protect it from excessive evaporation. On talus slopes and among rock rubble, where its roots can be shaded, though its leaves are in the sun, is the parsley fern (*Cryptogramma crispa*); its smooth, bright green leaves are of two types, both reminiscent of parsley.

Coltsfoot (Petasites frigidus)

Devil's Club (Oplopanax horridum)

One of the first plants to bloom in early spring; thick stalks topped by pink composite flower heads may cover cutbanks along a wooded highway before its leaves appear. As the flower stem elongates from a few inches to a foot, the leaves develop on separate stalks, reaching by summer a diameter of a foot or so. Leaves on the plants in the picture are just beginning to grow. Coltsfoot is also found in such places as disturbed earth along a streambank; it requires somewhat moist conditions. It is one of our native (many roadside plants are introduced) pioneer plants, that is, one which seems to be adapted to colonizing newly-opened ground. Seeds, like those of fireweed, are light as well as winged, undoubtedly a big advantage enabling them often to get there first. Patches are formed by creeping rhizomes (rootstocks or underground stems).

A variety found at high elevations has smaller leaves, less deeply lobed. It, too, grows by streams. Less conspicuous in flower, it may be noticed most when in seed; the shiny silky balls, just before they blow away, are much neater than the unkempt lowland relative at this stage.

The variety pictured, listed in the past as *P. speciosus*, extends up to moderate elevations in the Cascades.

Photographed in May alongside a logging road on French Ridge near Darrington, on High Speed Ektachrome with a 35mm Canon.

Devil's Club

Oplopanax horridum (Ginseng Family)

A shrub of damp ravines, well-watered riverbanks, places where soil is deep and moisture is close to the surface all season. If you grab one of these for support while climbing over a log, you find out why loggers named it devil's club. Finger-thick stems appear thicker and club-shaped at the top because of the mass of spines. Small greenish blossoms are not much noticed, but colorful berries are first yellow and orange, finally a bright scarlet red. Leaves are often a foot across, making it a dramatic shrub with possibilities in landscaping. After the leaves have fallen, the thick size of the stems makes it possible to tell devil's club from the pencil-thin spiny stems of salmonberry or gooseberry.

One of the specimens first collected by Archibald Menzies at Nootka Sound on Vancouver Island, devil's club ranges from Alaska to southern Oregon, and eastward in British Columbia and northern Washington to Idaho and Montana. This distribution pattern is found in a number of species, corresponding with storm and weather patterns bringing coastal moisture inland. Devil's club is prominent in western valley approaches to the Cascades, often associated with western red cedar, maidenhair and other ferns, yellow violet (*Viola glabella*), corydalis.

Despite the fact that the leaves are prickly underneath, it is said they are eaten by elk. A related large-leaved plant of California is called elk clover, a correlation it would be interesting to explore further.

Berries are colorful in late summer; note the dry, yellowed moss on the tree trunks. Foliage visible includes sword and oak ferns and vine maple.

Photographed in August on the Mountain Loop Highway near Verlot, with a 4x5-inch Super Graphic.

Above, Foamflower (Tiarella unifoliata). Right, Vanilla Leaf (Achlys triphylla)

In cool, shady forests, sometimes so dense that little else grows, foamflower's tiny white starry blossoms brighten the forest floor through middle and late summer. Foamflower has a long period of bloom; in the photograph it can be noted that there are seed capsules on the lower part of the stem, flowers higher, and buds near the top. The airy inflorescence is of a type called a panicle — side-branches branch again to hold the flowers.

The picture was taken on the trail to the Grove of the Patriarchs, a group of forest giants. The fern leaf in the center attests to the moist conditions required by the foamflower, whose own bristly three-lobed leaves show around the edges of the photograph.

Another foamflower, *T. trifoliata,* differing only in that its leaves are three-parted rather than lobed, is so similar that most people will take little note. Both plants have smaller flowers than the foamflower of eastern woods, *T. cordifolia.* Rather similar leaves, but various blossoms are found in a great many other plants in the saxifrage family: the fringecup (*Tellima*), youth-on-age (*Tolmiea*), several alumroots (*Heuchera*), mitreworts (*Mitella*), and *Boykinia.* A third Northwest foamflower, with deeply-slashed leaves, is more of a coastal woods plant. Some botanists consider these three just one species.

Foamflower growing along the Ohanapecosh River trail (in the southeast corner of Mount Rainier National Park), photographed on a rainy June day with a 4x5-inch Super Graphic camera.

Vanilla Leaf

Achlys triphylla **(Barberry Family)**

Like the foamflower, vanilla leaf is a shade-tolerant species of the deep forest, but found under maple or alder as well as various conifers. It grows only in the Northwest. When dried the leaves have a fragrance reminiscent of vanilla; pioneer women used them for their linen storage. Fishermen find the large fresh leaves appropriate for wrapping trout.

Spreading widely by rhizomes (underground stems), the plants may form large patches, particularly on stream benches (the flowers pictured grew beside the Skagit River). The three-parted leaf on a long, wiry stalk neatly fits together to form a circular outline. Flowers are in a crowded spike atop a separate wiry stem, 8 to 16 inches tall. They have no sepals or petals but consist solely of the essentials, stamens and stigmas. Small round fruits are a sort of purplish color.

Botanists have assigned this plant to the barberry family. It does not much resemble the large shrubby members; family relationships are based, not on a plant's general form, rather on flower parts, in this case very minute and so not easily seen. Besides the well-known Oregon grapes of several species, one of which is Oregon's state flower, another interesting Northwest member of the family is the inside-out flower, *Vancouveria hexandra*. Named after Captain George Vancouver, it is similar in size to the vanilla leaf, has tough rather than tender stems and leaves, the twice three-parted leaves are comparatively small, and white petals are sharply reflexed.

Vanilla leaf photographed at Rockport State Park near Marblemount, using a 4x5-inch camera. Picture was taken during a few minutes of sunshine between heavy rain showers. There is a good display of this flower at the foot of the giant fir tree in the Grove of the Patriarchs at Ohanapecosh in Mount Rainier National Park.

27

Left, Bleeding Heart (Dicentra formosa). Above, Yellow Violet (Viola glabella)

The heart is easy to see; its bleeding is more easily understood in the old-fashioned garden flower, *Dicentra spectabilis,* which has a valentine shape plus an extended bit of petal just the right proportion to form a drop at one stage of flower development. The intricate blossom consists of four petals. The outer pair are spurred (the bag shape at the top), folded, and divergent at the tip (bent outwards at the bottom). They meet so neatly that hardly any line shows, except at the bottom where they part just enough to show a glimpse of the plainer inner pair. The unsuspecting reader might be warned before tackling technical manuals that in scientific description the top of this heart is the base, botanists having agreed that the end at which petals are attached to the stalk is their base, thus providing themselves with a word they can use whether the flower faces up, down, or sidewards, or begins by nodding and finishes erect, as some do.

Succulent, leafless stems, around a foot in height, hold the flowers just above the bed of ferny leaves, sometimes covering a large area in moist, shady places. Found from lowlands, where it is a late spring flower, up to middle elevations in the mountains.

A close relative, *Dicentra uniflora,* is a tiny ground-hugging plant with a washed-out pink flower that has long curved outer petals and a skinny central part resembling nothing so much as the skull of a longhorn steer, and aptly called steer's head. It may be found at middle elevations on the eastern slopes of the Cascades, in loose soil on sunny exposures, blooming soon after the snow leaves. Other *Dicentras* include the Dutchman's breeches and squirrel corn of eastern United States. The scientific name comes from the Greek, meaning twice-spurred.

Bleeding heart photographed in May near the top of MacDonald Lookout near Enumclaw. Taken on a bright day, in the shaded forest, with a 4x5-inch Super Graphic.

Yellow Violet *Viola glabella* (Violet Family)

Yellow violets outnumber purple ones in the Cascades, though the color popularly associated with violets is found in some mountain meadows. *Viola glabella* is perhaps most common, and can be recognized by its erect, leafy blossom stems with flowers near the top, and bright green leaves, pointed at the outer end, not evergreen. Typical of damp places, found at various elevations with such flowers as bleeding heart, trillium, salmonberry, and growing rapidly, it frequently forms large colonies by a streambank where periodic flooding leaves new ground open. Surprisingly enough, it is also found on open mountain slopes where grass and other vegetation are not too thick, though it cannot compete with grassy sod where the dark blue-purple *Viola adunca* grows.

Two evergreen yellow violets divide the same elevation span, one growing in low-elevation woods, the other in the upper forest and also in the lowest meadows, where it is associated with avalanche lily, heather, and spring beauty. Both have leaves rounded in outline, most appearing to originate near ground level. Another yellow, with shiny, gray leaves, very irregularly shaped, is found on drier eastside slopes; both leaves and petals are backed with purple.

A variety of unused names have been proposed for *Viola glabella*. For those who wish to be specific in referring to yellow violets, tall yellow violet is suggested by the author as an easily remembered name that would distinguish this one from other yellow violets in the Northwest. (The scientists have a little trouble with names also; all four have names whose meanings could apply to others. Therefore, the much-used, easy way of creating an instant "common" name by translating from the scientific one is not much help with violets.)

Photographed in early May in the foothills of the Cascades just east of Vancouver, Washington. Taken with a 4x5-inch camera, between rain showers, in very hazy sunlight.

Coralroot (Corallorhiza mertensiana)

No leaves, no chlorophyll, yet its flowers brighten dense, shady coniferous forests. This particular species of coralroot is often seen where there is little other undergrowth on the needle-covered forest floor. It is a saprophyte, dependent for its food upon decomposed plant materials, partially upon certain fungi growing with it and decomposing woody materials in the ground. Adapted to live in this same way, therefore not bothered by a shortage of sunlight, are other *Corallorhiza* species, members of the orchid family, as well as Indian pipe and several additional members of the heath family.

Corallorhiza mertensiana is our most common Northwest coralroot, found typically in the lower montane zone in dry woods. Its lip (downward-pointing flower part) is splotched with such a large amount of purple that it is usually described as being purple with irregular white markings. It cannot be confused with the striped coralroot, *C. striata,* whose perianth parts (three sepals and three petals) are all candy-striped, inside and out. The spotted coralroot, seen only occasionally here, is a different brown-purple shade, and can be recognized by the polka-dotted lip. Its species name, *C. maculata,* means spotted and is most apt, the large petal being sprinkled with small dark dots. If it is seen, it will be easily recognized; in the meantime assume, since other people have walked in the Cascades for 10 years before seeing anything but, that you are looking at *C. mertensiana.*

Coralroots are about 8 inches tall. It is not uncommon for pale yellow forms of either *C. maculata* or *C. mertensiana* to be found growing in a patch of the typical purple plants.

Photographed on a cloudy day in late June along the Van Trump trail, Mount Rainier National Park, with a Canon 35mm camera on Kodachrome II film. Good places to see coralroot include the Owyhigh Lakes trail on the White River side of Mount Rainier and the Commonwealth Basin trail near Snoqualmie Pass.

Coralroots received their name from the coral-like rhizome or rootstock, an underground portion of stem, which in these plants is much branched and knobby. Above-ground clusters of flower stalks growing close together probably come from the same rhizome.

Corallorhiza mertensiana was named after Carl H. Mertens, naturalist with Friedrich Luetke's Russian ship sent out from St. Petersburg to chart Alaskan waters in the 1820s. This man is commemorated also in the specific names of two other plants widespread in western America, the mountain hemlock, *Tsuga mertensiana,* and the white heather, *Cassiope mertensiana,* as well as a small saxifrage and a sedge, all first described scientifically from specimens collected at Sitka, Alaska. Luckier than some of our other Northwest botanical explorers, Mertens apparently is in no danger of being forgotten. Many taxonomists (botanical specialists who assign names to plants) have had the habit of naming plants after their friends or people who collected specimens for them, but the rules of the game are such that the names do not always stick. It depends upon whether other taxonomists recognize the plant as truly a new species or decide it belongs instead with some other species already described and named. Another common practice was to name a plant after the place where it was collected; our Cascades valerian, for example, is *Valeriana sitchensis* (a latinized form of Sitka). When we find these names attached to one of our plants, it has a range at least from southeast Alaska to Washington, quite possible on down to northwest California.

Photographed on the first of July on Pilot Ridge near Darrington, with sunlight streaming through the forest. 35mm Canon on Kodachrome II film.

Left, Linnaea or Twinflower (Linnaea borealis). Above, Clintonia or Queen's Cup (Clintonia uniflora)

Linnaea; Twinflower

Linnaea borealis (Honeysuckle Family)

A creeping evergreen found in a variety of forest situations, moist to dry, sealevel to lower subalpine elevations, but perhaps at its best in drier sites in our climate. May form quite large carpets. Paired flowers, nodding from a Y-forked stem, are soft pink velvet inside. Other parts of the plant may also be more or less hairy, as shown in the slightly-enlarged photograph, but the leaves usually give an impression of smoothness.

Carolus Linnaeus, Swedish physician, botanist, and teacher, wrote in 1737 that if you do not know names for things, your knowledge of them is lost. A very observant man who loved flowers and described himself as a "born methodizer," he began making descriptive lists of plants of the countryside and soon determined to do something about their names, which varied with each authority consulted. He proposed a system of double names, taken from Latin or Greek, with which all educated Europeans of the time were acquainted, one for the genus to show close relationships, and a following name to distinguish the particular species. He recommended keeping old Greek and Latin names for genera and coining other necessary ones from mythology or to commemorate kings and famous botanists. For species names he recommended using some unique characteristic which distinguished this one from all other members of the genus, thus making it easy to associate name with plant. The linnaea was his favorite plant and for this reason named after him; he held a sprig of it whenever his portrait was painted and included it in his coat of arms when he was knighted for his scientific contributions. Linnaeus' binomial system, adopted internationally, is still in use today, and recognized scientific names for plants and animals are the same all over the world.

Linnaea, also called twinflower, is circumboreal, being found in northern Eurasian forests, prominent in the northern spruce-balsam forest of North America, and also a common plant in the upper montane forest of the Rockies. Northwestern plants have in the past been listed under *L. longiflora*.

Photographed during a rainstorm in late May on the Ohanapecosh River trail, with a 4x5-inch Super Graphic camera. Good places to find twinflower include the first mile or two up the White River trail, as well as the Carbon River valley in Mount Rainier National Park and along the Entiat River near the Larch Lakes trail.

Clintonia; Queen's Cup

Clintonia uniflora (Lily Family)

Two or three glossy leaves with parallel veining suggesting the lily family, and growing out of their center a slender stem with a single pure white flower on top—it often forms large colonies carpeting the underground. There is a creeping rhizome or ground stem. This clintonia is one of the common flowers of montane forests, ranging from southern Alaska through the Cascades to the Sierra, also in the Olympics and Oregon Coast Range, as well as east to Montana and the Canadian Rockies.

The genus was named after DeWitt Clinton, a naturalist and early governor of New York, who promoted the building of the Erie Canal. The members are forest plants, apparently shade-tolerant. Color of the flowers varies, some being greenish-yellow, one red; most have numerous flowers on a stem. Three species, including ours, have metallic blue fruits shaped like beads, which accounts for a common name of beadlily. The name queen's cup was given by Julia Henshaw of Vancouver, British Columbia, when she wrote a mountain flower book in 1915; some whose sympathies lie not with royalist traditions have opposed this one. As botanical names go, clintonia is euphonius and easy to pronounce, but objectors on political grounds go all the way back to Henry Thoreau. Though names are interesting, in this case it may be better not to know their origin.

A number of other forest flowers have interesting berries in late summer. The Canadian dogwood gets its alternate name of bunchberry from the cluster of red berries surrounded by a circle of leaves. The white-flowered twisted stalk has elongated, translucent red berries hanging below its leafy branches, and those of the rosy twisted stalk are round. Fairy bells have orange berries which are opaque.

Photographed in early June on the Lost Creek Ridge trail, west of Glacier Peak, with a 4x5-inch Super Graphic camera. A dense forest shaded the otherwise bright sunlight. The photographers have also seen especially good displays of queen's cup on the Schriebers Meadow trail near Mount Baker in early July and along the trail to Summerland in August.

Corydalis (Corydalis scouleri)

Corydalis (Corydalis scouleri)

Corydalis scouleri (Fumitory Family)

Pronounce it with a riddle in the middle and the accent on the "ryd." Corydalis of various colors will be familiar to many gardeners. The kinds that are cultivated are much more compact than this one, which grows 2 to 4 feet tall. Like the bleeding heart and other members of the family, it has fast-growing, tender stems with a lot of water in them. The stems are easily broken and leaves wilt quickly. Flowers differ from the bleeding heart in that only one petal is spurred. The blooming season is a long one in the sense that new flowers are still coming out on the top of the raceme while seeds have already formed at the bottom. When seeds are ripe in midsummer, pods are triggered with a spring which, when brushed by a passerby, shoots the seeds some distance from the plant.

It may be called Scouler corydalis to distinguish it from some hundred other kinds growing in various parts of the world. Dr. John Scouler, who also has a bluebell, a willow, and a fern named after him, assisted David Douglas with plant collecting in 1825, working with him near the mouth of the Columbia River and around Fort Vancouver in the spring, and then going by boat up to Nootka Sound and back, stopping at various harbors along the way. He found this plant plentiful near the mouth of the Columbia. Common in moist places in valley forests, particularly at Mount Rainier; not much seen northward; also found in the Olympics and in the coastal region.

The fumitory family is named after the common fumitory, a European annual weed of arable lands, which it may infest thickly enough to smother seedling crops. Formerly used in medicine as a blood purifier, its name comes from the Latin "fumus," smoke.

Photographed on a dark day in the woods alongside the Wonderland Trail near the North Puyallup River, in July, with a 35mm Canon camera and High Speed Ektachrome film.

The dense forests are often quite still; wildlife is not plentiful and most of what there is keeps well hidden. Two birdsongs, however, are associated with the deep woods. The cheery bubbling song of the winter wren comes from bushes close to the ground, where this small dark bird finds most of the insects it eats; it builds its nest among roots on the forest floor. This wren is found across Canada and is also the Jenny Wren of English song and story, being the only one found in Eurasia.

The varied thrush is a more elusive singer, a long, single whistled note being repeated at intervals in different tones from the top of some conifer the hiker cannot see because of the thickness of the forest. Usually it is difficult to place the exact direction from which the song is coming. Early summer is the time when this thrush will be heard. In winter, when it migrates downward like the winter wren, but even closer to people's homes, the varied thrush may be recognized by its similarity to a robin but with a black band across its breast. It is a northwestern bird.

Photographed in the open on the Klapatche-North Puyallup River section of the Wonderland Trail in Mount Rainier National Park. This was taken with a 35mm Canon camera on High Speed Ektachrome film, on the same day as the other picture of this flower on the opposite page. Corydalis can also be seen on the trail to Spray Park and on trails in the Carbon River valley.

Left, Pink Pyrola (Pyrola asarifolia).

Above, Sidebells Pyrola (Pyrola secunda)

Europeans call these plants wintergreens in reference to the leaves which remain green over winter. Americans have used the name wintergreen for a different plant, *Gaultheria procumbens,* from whose leaves the familiar wintergreen flavoring is derived. The resulting confusion gives us little choice but to plunge in and learn to pronounce the scientific name if we wish to have people understand to what plant we refer. The accent is on the "peer"; the name is taken from the Latin for little pear, supposedly referring to the shape of the leaves.

Pyrola asarifolia is common in the Cascades and easily recognized by the combination of pink flowers and large green leaves. The style forms an unusual-looking appendage, first bending abruptly downward, then curving upward. Some other species of pyrolas are distinguished by their straight styles: *P. secunda* and *P. uniflora,* which are pictured elsewhere in this book.

Those of ours with flowers similar to the one shown here may be told apart by their different types of leaves. *Pyrola picta* has dark green leaves with pale streaks, white to pinkish flowers; *P. dentata* has pale or bluish-green leaves of an oblong shape and creamy-white flowers; both are northwesterners. *P. virens* has comparatively small leaves and greenish-yellow flowers; it is more widely distributed. Occasionally some will be found without leaves at all—they are considered to belong to one or another of these species, but since it is not easy to decide which, they are called *P. aphylla* ("without leaves").

Pyrola asarifolia may be found listed in other books as *P. bracteata* and *P. ulignosa;* all are considered one species by the latest authorities. Since this is the most definitely pink-flowered one, it seems appropriate to call it the pink pyrola.

Taken in early July at the start of the Owyhigh Lakes trail, Mount Rainier National Park; bright sunshine shaded by trees. With 35mm Canon camera on High Speed Ektachrome film.

Sidebells Pyrola

Pyrolas are found particularly in coniferous woods. This one is common in the Cascades in the montane or Canadian life zone, and ranges also from Alaska to California, east to Greenland and New England, as well as in Europe and Asia. It receives its name from the one-sided raceme of flowers, unique among the pyrolas. It is further distinguished from most others in the genus by the straight style and the leaves growing partway up the stem. In comparison with the preceding pink pyrola, it is generally smaller. The blooms are always a sort of greenish color, blending with the rest of the plant.

Pyrola minor is another with a straight style. Its small leaves, however, are all basal and the small, pink-flushed flowers grow on all sides of the stem. Though rare here, it is the so-called common wintergreen of Norway and northern Britain.

These species both being found, along with *P. virens* and *P. unifolia,* in northern conifer forests around the world, it is interesting to speculate why. It has been suggested that a mycorhizal partnership with root fungi which absorb dead organic matter from the soil, a common trait in the heath family, may have some bearing. Since bacterial decay is slow in the low temperatures characteristic of the boreal forest, this way of unlocking needed nutrients gives such a plant an advantage. Tree species vary in different areas of this belt, but forest conditions are similar, and a number of other flowers also are circumboreal.

Some authors use the term montane to describe forested slopes on mountains at a level intermediate between lowland or foothill forests and subalpine ones.

Sidebells pyrola photographed on the Owyhigh Lakes trail in early July; 35mm Canon camera, High Speed Ektachrome film.

Salal (Gaultheria shallon)

Red Huckleberry (Vaccinium parvifolium)

Menziesia (Menziesia ferruginea)

Salal

One of the most common Northwest shrubs west of the Cascade crest, salal is ordinarily 3 to 6 feet tall, but may be reduced to a foot or less as it ascends partway up the mountains. Attractive, shiny, and leathery leaves are familiar as greens used by florists. The flowers, white flushed with pink, have the same closed bell or urn shape as many other members of the heath family, such as madrona, manzanita, kinnikinnick, and huckleberry.

Later come black-purple berries which are utilized by a number of animals. These "berries" are different from most, being formed by a thickened and pulpy calyx, rather than the usual enlargement of the ovary walls. There is a many-seeded capsule, or pod, inside. Where salal grew in abundance, Northwest Indians made large cakes of mashed, dried berries to store for winter.

The pioneers also used this fruit in pies and jelly, often mixed with other berries for a more desirable flavor, since not everyone enjoys salal straight. Leaves are browsed by deer, especially in summer. Two miniature-shrub species of higher elevations have bright red berries.

The name salal comes from the Chinook word for the berries. The genus is named after Jean Gaultier, a physician and botanist of early-day Quebec. One of the *Gaultherias* from eastern America has aromatic leaves from which is obtained oil of wintergreen used in flavoring and medicine.

Photographed in early June, in sunshine, on the Trail of the Shadows at Longmire, with a 35mm Canon camera on Kodachrome II.

Red Huckleberry

Taken in mid-August on Backbone Ridge, Mount Rainier, with 35mm Canon camera on High Speed Ektachrome film.

Like the salal, red huckleberry often takes root on rotten logs or snags, seeds planted in the higher spots by a bird or some animal like a chipmunk that ate the berry. Potentially a tall plant, its leaves are small compared with most other huckleberries, accounting for the name "parvifolium", which means small-leaved. Photographed in larger proportions than the two shrubs shown with it, the red huckleberry leaves are less than an inch long, and berries just a little larger than their flowers. Grouse huckleberry, *V. scoparium*, with very tiny red berries, is a similarly green-stemmed but low plant often seen as a ground cover with lodgepole pine or in other fairly dry montane situations, and more common on the east side of the Cascades.

Leaves are arranged in a circular plane, similarly to those of rhododendron and Labrador tea, not lengthwise along the stem as are huckleberry leaves. Even when there are no blossoms it should be relatively easy to tell them. A more technical distinction is in the position of the ovary, superior in the menziesia, meaning it is inside the flower and invisible in the picture; in huckleberries it is inferior, the thickened part at the base of the flower showing where the berry is going to grow (see photograph of huckleberry blossom, p. 184). Menziesia is found in mixed shrubby undergrowth, often with several of the tall huckleberries, 2 to 6 feet tall.

The shrub was named after Archibald Menzies, surgeon with George Vancouver's and other British expeditions to the northwest coast of America in the 1790s, and the first botanist to visit this area. He collected extensively at Nootka Sound and also picked specimens as far north as Prince William Sound, Alaska, as well as in California. As was customary, many of the plants were named after the collector who brought them back. Besides this genus, new species named after Menzies included the madrona, several mosses, a delphinium, a pipsissewa, and Douglas fir, the twin commemoration for the last being an example of how names got doubled up when several scientists working with materials from different collectors named the same plant. Among other plants collected by Menzies were the western red cedar, our pink-flowered rhododendron, red and black huckleberries, vanilla leaf and vancouveria, clintonia, *Pyrola picta,* marsh marigold, and red heather.

There are six or seven species of menziesia, one growing in the Smokies and several in Japan. The name "ferruginea" means rust-colored, which could refer to the blossoms or may have been given because of the soft brownish hairs on the leaves. Rusty menziesia is sometimes listed as a common name for this shrub.

Photographed in July on the shore of Lake George, Mount Rainier; with 35mm Canon camera on High Speed Ektachrome film.

Left, Indian Pipe (Monotropa uniflora). Above, Pinesap (Hypopitys monotropa)

Indian pipe has no real leaves and no chlorophyll, the green matter that enables plants to manufacture food from sunlight, carbon dioxide, and water; it is a saprophyte, drawing nourishment from decaying organic matter, in conjunction with a mycorhizal fungus. Having no requirement for sunlight as an energy source, it can and does live in deep shade, and in fact, soon dies if the trees fall or are cut. In the Northwest, found in low-level forests only, so becoming very rare, as any plant must when its habitat disappears. A plant of deep, moist woods, in rich humus, from Alaska to Labrador, south to Mexico, not anywhere common.

The whole plant is first a waxy white, with a single nodding flower forming the "pipe." It blackens with age, and the stem straightens as the seedpod is formed; the seeds inside are tiny, like particles of dust.

Most observers will have a short list of places where they have discovered it. The author has seen it at Goldmeyer Hot Springs up the Middle Fork of the Snoqualmie River. The photographers, who hunted for it a long time, have also seen it on Sulphur Mountain near Darrington.

Photographed on the side of Tumtum Peak in Mount Rainier National Park, with a 4x5-inch Super Graphic.

Pinesap

Hypopitys monotropa (Heath Family)

Its range in America is similar to that of Indian pipe; it is found in addition in Europe. In the Northwest, pinesap grows at higher elevation levels, and at this point in time is a great deal more common. Though many of the characteristic forest shrubs persist in cutover land, and some flowers hang on with them, so continuing to grow in the regenerating forest, saprophytes such as pinesap and Indian pipe disappear quickly when forests are cut. Presumably they would come in again only when conditions are right and if there is a near enough seed source. Pinesap in the Cascades is usually pinkish with some underlying tawny or tan color; in some of its area, particularly Europe, it is yellow. It grows in forest litter, in somewhat drier sites than Indian pipe, and for a short part of the day may even please the photographer by standing in a shaft of sunlight.

Probably it is the only plant with a reversible name. Linnaeus put it in the same genus as the Indian pipe, with the species name "hypopitys," taken from Greek, referring to the plant's growth under firs. When it was decided it should have a genus of its own, the name was reversed as above, the species name then indicating it was very like the Indian pipe. Now some botanists are turning it around again, and in many current books you will find it listed as *Monotropa hypopitys*. When classified with the Indian pipe this way, the plant is sometimes called many flowered Indian pipe. In older books the name *Hypopitys lanuginosa* was also used for our western plants.

Photographed along the trail to Owyhigh Lakes in early July, with a 4x5-inch Super Graphic.

Rosy Twisted Stalk (Streptopus roseus)

Woodnymph (Pyrola uniflora)

Pipsissewa (Chimaphila umbellata)

Rosy Twisted Stalk

Streptopus roseus (Lily Family)

Photographed on the Tomyhoi Lake trail near Mount Baker, in June; with a 35mm Canon on High Speed Ektachrome.

This twisted stalk is found at middle (montane) elevations in moist, rich soil, mixed with a lot of other flowers. Tiny blossoms, here somewhat enlarged, are hidden under the leaves and may be noticed most easily if growing on a bank at eye level. Round berries are a bright translucent red.

S. streptopoides, a similar plant with saucer-shaped flowers and the same sort of berries, is not as important. These two are unbranched. A third species, the white-flowered twisted stalk, taller and usually with branching stems, has a right-angle turn in its flower stalk (pedicel), and its berries are long bead-shaped. Fairybells (*Disporum* species) are similar liliaceous plants with branching stems, but no twists in the pedicels.

S. roseus in the Northwest has been listed as *S. curvipes*.

Woodnymph

Pyrola uniflora (Heath Family)

Photographed in July on the Owyhigh Lakes trail with a 4x5-inch Super Graphic.

Woodnymph usually grows in mossy woods, some authorities say on rotting wood. Not an abundant plant, but widely distributed in cooler parts of North America and the Old World (circumboreal). Its five spreading white petals form a star-shaped flower, quite different in appearance from other pyrolas. Botanists have sometimes assigned it a separate genus, then naming it *Moneses uniflora*. Perhaps because it is rare in England, it has no really common English name; books have usually listed translations of the scientific name, either one-flowered wintergreen (*Pyrola*) or single delight (*Moneses*). The Norwegians call it Olavsstake, Olaf's candlestick—turn up the flower to see the resemblance.

Pipsissewa

Pipsissewa is found where the understory includes lots of moss, a sparse shrub cover, and very few herbaceous plants—a somewhat dry forest, most often at middle elevations. It is late blooming for a forest plant, often seen in August. The flowers look as though molded out of wax and center parts are jewel-like when viewed with a hand lens. Some people are reminded of a ballerina's skirt. Note that this species has dark green, shining leaves, widest toward the outer half. Another, less common species, Menzies pipsissewa, has fewer leaves, which are widest toward the base (nearest the stem) and faintly marked with light-colored streaks.

Waxy leaves of pipsissewa may serve to retard evaporation, possibly enabling the plant to cope with dry sites and acid soils. It has spreading rootstocks but does not form thick patches. It belongs to the same section of the heath family as the pyrolas. *C. umbellata*, the common pipsissewa, is another of the plants found round the world in northern latitudes. The common name comes from the Algonquian, the American origin a consequence of its not being found in England, though it does grow in Europe. That the plants of various areas are closely related is the view of present-day botanists. Formerly plants of western America have been listed as *C. occidentalis*.

Photographed on the South Fork Puyallup River trail, in Mount Rainier National Park, in late August Although there was a drizzle, the sky was quite bright and gave an excellent soft lighting. Taken with a 4x5-inch Super Graphic.

Above, Mertensia (Mertensia paniculata). Right, False Solomon's Seal (Smilacina racemosa)

One to 3 feet tall, this flower is found on streambanks and wet cliffs, in damp thickets and moist meadows. The plant is juicy and mountain beaver (*Aplodontia*) is particularly fond of it. Alpine chipmunks have been seen harvesting the seeds. *Mertensia paniculata* ranges from Alaska to Oregon and Quebec, from foothills to high meadows. Though other species are found at lower elevations on either side, this is the one which grows in the Cascade Mountains. It has also been listed under *M. laevigata*.

Flowers are shaped like blue bells with a long handle; they are often called bluebells, but there are many other bluebells. The name lungwort, sometimes seen, comes from the English name for a related plant, *Pulmonara officinalis*, which has spotted leaves and is grown in gardens here. The borage family also includes the familiar garden forget-me-nots, as well as the stickseeds (*Hackelia* species), native plants that look like forget-me-nots and have hooked burs which attach themselves to hikers' socks. The family is named after a European wildflower with bright blue, nodding, star-shaped flowers, borage (*Borago officinalis L.*). The L. following a scientific name in technical manuals means it was named by Linnaeus; officinalis means medicinal.

Like other members of the borage family, mertensia has one-sided flower clusters. They are often pink in bud. The genus was named after Professor Franz Mertens, botanist in Bremen, Germany, in the late 18th and early 19th centuries. Mertens coralroot, white heather, and mountain hemlock were named after another Mertens, his son Carl Heinrich, who collected the specimens at the Russian American Fur Company post at Sitka. Perhaps his father's prominence helped the young man gain a position as physician-naturalist on Luetke's surveying voyage in Alaskan waters in 1827.

Pictured on the Van Trump trail in Mount Rainier National Park. The photograph was taken on a wet, dark day in early July with a 35mm Canon camera on High Speed Ektachrome.

False Solomon's Seal   *Smilacina racemosa* (Lily Family)

False solomon's seal, like bleeding heart, trillium, and the yellow violet, *V. glabella,* is a lowland Washington plant that ascends quite high into the mountains. Occasional scattered clumps are found in shady or open, moist woods; not, apparently, where soil is acid. Only once does the author remember an extensive patch—this on Brush Creek, on the Cascade Crest Trail between Harts Pass and the North Cross-State Highway. The stem is tall and leafy. Tiny flowers are massed at the tip in a branching inflorescence, or panicle. The false solomon's seal is therefore easy to tell from the similar-leaved twisted stalks and fairy-bells, with blossoms under the leaves. Its berries are at first spotted, then red. The plant is usually 1½ or 2 feet tall.

Star-flowered false solomon's seal has fewer flowers, each on its own stalk; that is, a raceme, unbranched. Berries begin to ripen with wine-red stripes. A smaller, less showy plant, growing in patches, in moist woods to dry open hillsides.

The solomon's seal (*Polygonatum*) is another member of the lily family, similar in habit and leaf, but with blossoms hanging down all along the stem; it is not found in the Northwest. *Smilacina racemosa* and *S. stellata* grow through most of America. In the past, Northwest ones have been listed, respectively, as *S. amplexicaulis* and *S. sessilifolia.* They are also called solomonplume.

Photographed leaning, as it often does, over the Van Trump trail. Taken on a wet, dark day in early July with a 35mm Canon camera on High Speed Ektachrome.

Above, Creeping Raspberry (Rubus lasiococcus). Right, Fireweed (Epilobium angustifolium)

A creeping plant with frequently-rooting herbaceous stems, in the same genus with blackberries, raspberries, and salmonberry, though no more than a few inches tall, and unarmed. Red fruits are composed of several drupelets, looking like part of a raspberry. It is found at montane and subalpine levels.

The three-lobed leaves have a wrinkled texture. Another common one is *Rubus pedatus,* with flatter leaves that are five-parted (or three-parted with the lower two sections subdivided almost to the base; the general effect is the same). Their habitats are slightly different: one may walk through an open brushy area— slide or burn or ridgetop—with *R. lasiococcus,* go into the shady forest and see *R. pedatus.* Or find them growing on opposite sides of a ridge, *R. pedatus* requiring perhaps a more moist and shady microclimate. Temperatures are also more equable in the shelter of the trees because the forest floor is not as exposed to the wind. (A third species, *R. nivalis,* has prickly stems and is not as common in the Cascades.)

Another name is trailing rubus, often used particularly for *R. pedatus.* Technically, it is a creeping plant because the wandering stem puts down roots frequently which a trailing stem does not, but then, common names are apt to give more consideration to euphonics than technicalities. "Lasiococcus" means rough or hairy-fruited; "pedatus" means footed or bird-footed; "nivalis" means snowy. Translations of these species names are sometimes used when a precise name is wanted for each. The generic name bramble is also used sometimes, though they are not all prickly.

Photographed in the shade on a bank beside the trail, Napeequa Valley (Glacier Peak Wilderness Area), in August. With 35mm Canon camera on High Speed Ektachrome film. These were late flowers as most of the other plants of this species were through blooming.

Fireweed   *Epilobium angustifolium* (Evening Primrose Family)

Fireweed surprises us by how quickly it covers a piece of burntover land. The seeds are light and tiny, with a tuft of long, soft hairs enabling them to sail in the wind, but where do they come from? Sometimes the plant subsists for a very long time in the forest, not very vigorous, non-flowering, until fire gives it another chance to grow in the sun. Sprouting from root-stocks (conifers die if above-ground parts are killed), and stimulated by the increased light, fireweed is able to spread rapidly throughout the open area, both vegetatively and by producing lots of seeds. Fireweed spreads along cutbanks and logged areas even if they are not burned; not fussy about soil and moisture, it is an excellent example of a pioneer plant.

Pioneer plants often demand light and heat. As more plants come into the area the pioneers are shaded out, so their survival depends on fast production of many widely-dispersible seeds, getting in to colonize any area that happens to become bare. Some we know well as cosmopolitan weeds accompanying man's use of ground.

Other plants, in addition to fireweed, that tend to proliferate for a time in mountain burns include bracken fern, thimbleberry, trailing blackberry, several huckleberries, lupine, beargrass, snowbrush. Most of these are not considered pioneers, yet in a long view, their dominance in the area is only a temporary phase in the succession (which may take a few hundred years or more) leading again toward a similar sort of forest as that present before the fire.

Fireweed and 6120-foot Big Four Mountain on the Mountain Loop Highway near Silverton, taken with 35mm Canon camera on Kodachrome II film.

75

Salmonberry (Rubus spectabilis)

Marsh Violet (Viola palustris)

Shooting Star (Dodecatheon jeffreyi)

Salmonberry

This picture shows both the blossom and a berry in formative stage. Taken with 35mm Canon camera on High Speed Ekta-chrome film, on the Bedal Basin trail near Darrington, one of several on which salmon-berry overgrows miles of trail.

Magenta-pink flowers begin to bloom early, just as the leaves start to unfold. Berries ripen in midsummer, are a golden yellow or occasionally red, like a fat raspberry in shape. When they come off at a touch, they are ready to eat. A shrub of the moister parts of the Douglas fir-western hemlock forest, some of the flowers growing under it might be trillium, bleeding heart, the tall yellow violet, *V. glabella,* and at times, the marsh violet. Among the trees it grows as a tall, spindly shrub, spiny enough to avoid brushing against. When out in the open, it is quite aggressive, forming almost impenetrable thickets and apt to overgrow a trail rather quickly.

Salmonberry is found from Alaska to northwest California, mostly west of the Cascade crest; it was collected by Meriwether Lewis. The species name, "spectabilis," means showy or beautiful (in comparison with the ordinary white flowers of most blackberries and raspberries, which are also in the genus *Rubus*).

Marsh Violet

Viola palustris (Violet Family)

Marsh violets are the hidden sort. Their lavender or pale violet blossoms may be discovered in wet grassy patches, often under brush beside streams. Tiny white violets, *V. macloskeyi,* grow in similar saturated habitat, blooms scattered in the grass where only the sharpest eyes find them. Both have a wide elevation range. Marsh violet is sometimes listed as *Viola epipsila.*

Photographed in a marshy area along-side the Nooksack River near the Nooksack Cirque, in early June.

Shooting Star   *Dodecatheon jeffreyi* (Primrose Family)

Common on wet ground particularly along streams, in subalpine woods and meadows, often associated with marsh marigold and, like it, apparently inured to early-season cold floodwaters which may cover it blossoms and all. The petals are sharply reflexed (turned backwards) like those of the cyclamen, another member of the primrose family. Dark stamens closely surround the style to form a slender downward-pointing cone. The basal leaves grow upright in a circle around the stem. Grows from Alaska south in the mountains to California and east to Idaho and Montana. Occasionally, pure white specimens are seen.

Some flowers like the avalanche lilies droop sadly when it rains, but shooting stars and marsh marigolds are cheerfully firm even when covered with water. How do they keep their pollen from being washed away?

If it is desired to distinguish this one from others found in different areas, it may be called Jeffrey shooting star. John Jeffrey was a Scottish botanist sent out after David Douglas' death to supplement his work of collecting seeds of horticultural interest. In the early 1850s he worked from Fort Colville into British Columbia and in northern Washington including Mount Baker, then around Fort Nisqually and Fort Vancouver, before continuing his explorations southward. The Jeffrey pine of Oregon and California was also named after him. Apparently his 2 years of collecting had little other impact.

This species has also been listed under the name *D. viviparum.*

Photographed along the trail to Edith Creek basin at Paradise, Mount Rainier National Park. It was a windy day and despite wind screens erected around the flower, there was still movement. 35mm Canon camera on High Speed Ektachrome film.

79

Scarlet Gilia (Gilia aggregata)

Snowbrush (Ceanothus velutinus)

Except that they belong in the phlox family, botanists tend to disagree about the various plants that have at one time or another been included among gilias. The scarlet gilia, sometimes listed as *Ipomopsis aggregata,* is not found west of the Cascade crest in Washington, but is otherwise widespread in western United States, from lowland valleys almost to timberline. It is often seen on roadbanks or other fairly dry areas where vegetation is open.

The trumpet-shaped red flowers are attractive to hummingbirds. Though small in size, they make up for this by the large numbers upon each stalk and a tendency to form patches. Leaves of the scarlet gilia are divided into many narrow segments, and the plants are 1 or 2 feet tall. They are biennial; that is, they develop a leaf rosette the first year, and a blooming stalk the next, then having set seed to provide for the next generation, they die. As is true of most mountain plants, practically all the rest of the flowers pictured in this book are perennial.

Nuttall's gilia, a 3- or 4-inch plant with white flowers similar to those of phlox, and with contrasting orange anthers, grows on dry and rocky subalpine slopes and occasionally above timberline. Found south to the Sierras and east to the Rockies, its distribution at Mount Rainier seems peculiar in that it is more commonly seen on the stormy southwest side, as on top of Eagle Peak, and high in Van Trump and Klapatche Parks, rather than on the northeast side in the rain shadow of the mountain where it would seem that more dry habitat is available. It now has the tongue-twisting name of *Linanthastrum nuttallii.*

The first syllable of gilia is pronounced as in Jill.

Photographed in Swakane Canyon near Wenatchee in late May with a 35mm Canon camera on High Speed Ektachrome film. Also seen in the Fish Lake area the first of July and partway up the Paddy-Go-Easy trail above the lake in early August.

Snowbrush

Ceanothus velutinus (Buckthorn Family)

An aromatic shrub several feet tall, sometimes man-high, and tending to form thick patches. The leaves are sticky on top and shine as though just given a coat of varnish. In early summer the patches are topped with snowy clusters of bloom. Snowbrush grows in coastal areas and in the mountains on dry slopes. After a fire it may take over, not by means of wind-blown seeds like the fireweed, but if plants have been present they will sprout from the roots, and besides, hard seeds which have remained dormant in the shade are stimulated to germinate by heat, either from the fire or by the sun beating down directly on the ground.

This and some other ceanothus species are browsed by elk and deer. Ceanothus is an American genus with about 40 species, most abundant in California. The cascara, a small Northwest tree whose bark is gathered for its laxative properties, is also included in the buckthorn family. Neither snowbrush nor cascara are thorny, but many shrubs in the family are, and the family name comes from a European thorny one.

Another name for snowbrush is varnishleaf ceanthus. It is also called sticky laurel, though no relation to the classical laurel wreath, nor to the gardener's laurel hedge.

Photographed in early July on Dirty Face Mountain overlooking Lake Wenatchee; 35mm camera on High Speed Ektachrome film. Snowbrush is plentiful on McGregor Mountain near Stehekin and on Goat Peak in the Methow Valley.

83

Bog Orchid (Habenaria dilatata)

Marsh Marigold (Caltha biflora), two views

The white bog orchid is found in wet marshy places; look for it where trails cross drainage courses, among thick rank grasses and other plants, where the vegetation indicates an obviously wetter area than surrounding hillsides. This orchid is found over a wide range in North America and may grow as tall as 2 to 3 feet, but in the Cascades is more often about 6 to 10 inches high. There are several green-flowered bog orchids of similar size, growing in the same sort of habitat, more commonly really, but not so easily noticed as the white one.

Flowers of the orchid family are irregular in shape. The three outer parts (sepals) are usually much alike, colored and conspicuous. Two of the inner parts (petals) are alike and arranged laterally. The third inner one is different, usually very much so, mostly larger and of a distinctive shape, sometimes another color, often spurred; it is called the lip. The inferior ovary (placed below the petals and sepals) is usually long and twisted. In the bog orchids one sepal and the two lateral petals form a hood; the small flowers are arranged in long spikes, atop a leafy stem. Among the green ones, *Habenaria hyperborea* is distinguished by a long linear spur and a triangular lip like the white flower; *H. saccata* has a short, bag-shaped spur and a linear lip.

The bog orchids are closely related to a number of other plants which also may be classified as *Habenarias* or have sometimes been given other names. Included are the Alaska habenaria of dry open woods, whose basal leaves wither by flowering time, the fringed orchids of eastern North America, and others. Whether growing in wet or dry places, *Habenarias* are often called rein-orchis, a rough translation of the scientific name, which refers to the usually long, strap-shaped spurs.

Photographed on the edge of Fish Lake (in the Cle Elum valley) in mid-July, with a 35mm Canon camera on High Speed Ektachrome film.

Marsh Marigold

Banks of small streams, borders of ponds, marshy seepage areas of many kinds are favorite places for the marsh marigold to grow. Often in company with shooting star, but not typically in a mimulus garden, nor does it seem to join with the bog orchids. There are differences among the various wet habitats. Rather than the rocky or gravelly sort of stream where mimulus grows, marsh marigold roots in deep muck. Mimulus comes late, so requires a permanent water supply, a stream still running at the end of summer. Marsh marigold is an early bloomer, not minding temporary melt of rainwater floods, which sometimes cover even the blossoms. And like others in the buttercup family, the plant continues to grow after the flowers have faded, becoming tall and leggy.

There are two kinds. One, *Caltha leptosepala,* has leaves generally longer than broad, and grows around timberline or above. The other, *C. biflora,* has leaves broader than long; it may be found at slightly lower elevations, often in the woods. Both have gold-centered white flowers. In the northeastern Cascades globeflower grows in the same sort of wet situations; distinguish the leaves— sharp-toothed lobes on the outside edge of the globeflower's, rounded shape of the marsh marigold leaves. Fewer petals in the globeflower are another difference (technically both flowers have petaloid sepals, a sepal being an outer part, therefore first, while petals are not as important in the botanist's scheme of things).

Marsh marigolds growing in the mud of a melting snowpatch were photographed in late June on Round Mountain near Darrington. Both views taken with 35mm Canon camera on High Speed Ektachrome film.

Glacier Lily (Erythronium grandiflorum)

Glacier Lily (Erythronium grandiflorum)

Erythroniums are just a few in eastern North America and many in the west. This yellow species is wide-ranging, from British Columbia to Oregon and Colorado, from sagebrush slopes to treeline. In foothills of the Rockies and the east side of the Cascades it blooms while the calendar still says it is spring, coming soon after the snow is gone so sometimes called snow lily, especially in the Canadian Rockies. In mountain meadows the month is later, but still the glacier lily blooms immediately after the snow melts, or sometimes right through the snow.

Crocus and soldanella in the Swiss Alps, buttercup in the Rockies, glacier and avalanche lilies in the Cascades, in each mountain system there seem to be certain plants capable of blooming through the snow. While others wait until the soil is warmed to a certain degree, these plants are capable of growing at low temperatures, and their own metabolism generates heat.

The bits of needles and other debris blown onto the snow, as well as its granular form, indicate that old snow from the previous winter is pictured. Storms which deposit fresh snow may come at any time during the summer, covering all the mountain flowers with a short-lived mantle of cold slushy stuff.

Pale-anthered forms (the only sort found west of the Cascades, while elsewhere anthers may be dark red) have sometimes been listed as *E. pallidum*. The size varies around 6 inches.

On mountains in the western part of the Cascades the glacier lily appears noticeably the higher climber, and also is inclined toward earlier bloom than the white-flowered avalanche lily. And unlike the avalanche lily, it is not seen down in the west-slope subalpine forest. In a seeming paradox, it grows at much lower elevations east of the Cascade crest, lower than most of its high-country associates are found. This suggests that it may not be so much an adaptation to higher altitudes

Glacier lilies growing through the edge of melting snowbanks near Hannegan Pass (North Cascades), taken in early August with 4x5-inch Super Graphic.

and colder temperatures that keeps it from lower western slopes, as one might first suppose, rather something else.

Breaks with patches of avalanche lilies are sometimes abrupt, and glacier lilies may even prove to grow in sites that are warmer. Insolation is more intense at greater elevation, and daytime temperatures at ground level may be surprisingly high where exposed to full sun, particularly at certain angles, and when sheltered from the wind. Or, slightly drier conditions may turn out to be a decisive factor. The early blooming season may be possible because the particular slopes on which it grows receive slightly less total snow, keep less snow because of exposure to sun or wind, or are so steep and well-drained that snow disappears sooner.

Glacier lily blooms from March to August depending on elevation. Some years there is a bright patch of glacier lilies on the south side of Alta Vista in late May while the rest of Paradise Valley is still deep in snow. At about the same time they may be found blooming in the Cle Elum valley, on trails in the Icicle Creek area out of Leavenworth, and other places on the east side of the mountains. In addition to the Sunrise side of Mount Rainier, a good place to see them later is along the Lost Creek Ridge trail, east of Darrington, in early July.

This is another of the plant specimens brought back by Lewis and Clark. The name glacier lily is said to have been given because of its abundance in Glacier National Park.

Taken near White Pass (Glacier Peak Wilderness Area) in mid-July, on High Speed Ektachrome film. The 35mm camera was propped on the ground and steadied against a rock.

Buttercup (Ranunculus eschscholtzii), two views. Right, Avalanche Lily (Erythronium montanum)

Avalanche Lily

Erythronium montanum (Lily Family)

Masses of avalanche lilies lie so thick it seems there is little room for anything else, but as a matter of fact there is. The corms are deep in the ground, below the layer containing the main feeding roots of other meadow flowers and grasses. Leaves take advantage of the space in the sun at a different time; they begin to grow even before the snow has completely melted. The plants bloom quickly, the leaves do their work of photosynthesis, their product is stored in the corm for next year's leaves and blossoms, seeds are formed, and in a few weeks the leaves begin to fade. After that, it matters little if they are shaded by lupines and other meadow plants which develop later. The midseason hiker who learns to recognize the three-angled seedpod, widest at the top and tapering toward the stem end, will find them scattered among the later flowers. When in seed, though, it is not easy to say which were the white-flowered avalanche lilies, and which the yellow-flowered glacier lilies. Sometimes the pods disappear due to forays by the little alpine chipmunk.

If blossoms are found late in the season, it is likely to be a spot where snow was piled in a slow-melting drift or at the foot of an avalanche slope.

Why is it sometimes called avalanche fawnlily? Really what we are asking is, why did the fawn's mother ever let him get mixed up with an avalanche? *Erythroniums* are a conspicuous and appealing enough group of plants to have inspired a surfeit of names. To go back a bit, in colonial times settlers transferred names of flowers they had known in Europe to similar-appearing, not necessarily related ones they found in eastern North America. To distinguish native plants from those they brought with them to grow in their gardens—roses, cabbages, and others —they added prefixes such as wild or Indian. When a plant was sufficiently distinc-

Field of lilies photographed in late July on Mazama Ridge, in Mount Rainier National Park, with a 35mm Canon camera on Kodachrome II film. Paradise Valley and Spray Park are noted for avalanche lilies.

tive, or when no convenient name was available, a new name was sometimes coined. Sometimes there was a European species with an English name, but one not popularly known, or the American species did not enough resemble the Old World one to be recognized by the average person as a related plant, so a new name was made here. As settlers moved westward, coming into contact several times with entirely new sets of wild flowers, they took these different kinds of names with them, applying and reapplying them to plants along the way. Because of vast distances and poor communications apt names coined by inventive minds did not always spread as far as the flower grew.

Early in the 20th century a valiant attempt was made to unscramble this confusion of names, one flower being known by different names in various parts of the country, while a single name is often used for many widely-differing plants. A number of interested organizations joined forces to publish a book called *Standard Plant Names*. Borrowing the scientists' method the committee decided to assign one name to each genus and a distinguishing epithet for each species. In some cases an English name was made up based on the scientific name, hoping it would in time become a true popular name. These names relying so heavily on the then current state of taxonomical knowledge often seem meaningless now because the scientific names have been drastically revised. In other cases when no common name was found in either America or England, a name was constructed by using that of the most well-known species to stand for the genus, and adding to this a locally-used common name to distinguish another species. So we found ourselves struggling with the complicated concept of a small sheep and a young deer both associated with lily, and the lamb sticking his tongue out at us—lambstongue fawnlily for *Erythronium grandiflorum*. Since western mountain *Erythroniums* do not have the spotted leaves of their eastern relatives, there is not much here to relate the name to the flower. The simpler common names coined in the Northwest seem easier to remember, glacier lily for the yellow one, avalanche lily for the white.

Western Anemone (Anemone occidentalis)

Blue Violet (Viola adunca)

Lomatium (Lomatium species)

Phlox forms loose mats with scattered leaves, the ¾-inch flowers much the more conspicuous part of the plant and carpeting the ground. The soft leaves are needle-shaped; the flowers are pale pink, pale lavender, white, or faintly tinged with blue, and the color seems to fade out quickly. Phlox grows in open, sunny situations, on crumbling cliffs, pumice, and other loose or coarse, dry soils. Probably where the snow melts comparatively early. It blooms early in the summer, a little later at higher elevations.

This species is found from moderate to high elevations, in the mountains of southern Vancouver Island, in the Olympics, Saddle Mountain in northwestern Oregon, in the Cascades from southern British Columbia through Oregon to the Sierra Nevada in California, east through northern Washington and Idaho to northwestern Montana west of the Continental Divide, and in the mountains of northeastern Oregon. Distinguishing names for it include spreading phlox, which translates the scientific name, and creeping phlox, which differentiates it from the more cushion-form or taller upright species of the eastern Washington sagebrush area, though not from phloxes of other places.

Plants which can stand living in full sun often also require lots of light, so if taller plants come in and cast too much shade, the former will die out. Phlox is not commonly found in the lush, thick, moist meadow community, except perhaps at a trail edge.

An unrelated plant sometimes confused with phlox is moss campion, in the pink family. It, however, forms thick rounded cushions of dark green leaves, the flowers are smaller and a dark pink shade. It is strictly a high alpine plant.

Phlox photographed on Desolation Peak on the east side of Ross Lake, in early July, with a 35mm Canon on High Speed Ektachrome.

Blue Violet

Viola adunca (Violet Family)

The blue violet, *Viola adunca*, is found in scattered locations in mountain meadows as well as at sealevel. The meadows, typically grassy, range from dry to moist, often are located on warm south slopes. Deep violet, blue, or purple, the flowers are bluer than those of the marsh violet. Besides the drier, sunnier habitat, they are also distinguished by the prominent white beard on the lateral petals, and light centers. This species ranges through much of western America and east to the Atlantic coast. In some places found in woods, it is conspicuously absent from Cascade forests between the lowland and subalpine situations where it grows in the Northwest.

Photographed in mid-July near Union Gap in the Stevens Pass area with a 35mm Canon on High Speed Ektachrome film.

Lomatium

Lomatium species (Parsley Family)

Many species of *Lomatium* grow in arid parts of the West. Three in the Cascades have yellow flowers and long, narrow leaf segments like those pictured: *L. brandegei*, *L. triternatum*, and *L. ambiguum*. The first, found only in the northeastern part of the Cascades and the Wenatchee Mountains has nodding fruits; the other two are more widespread and have erect fruits. Our others with similar flowers have either more finely-dissected leaves or rather broad segments.

Lomatiums are often called desert parsley or spring gold, while some, because of fleshy roots once much used by the Indians, are called biscuitroot or by their Indian name of cous. These growing in the Cascades are not particularly productive. They are found on dry, frequently rocky slopes, in the open, and bloom relatively early, adding height as they do so.

Photographed in early July on Desolation Peak above Ross Lake, with a 35mm Canon camera on High Speed Ektachrome film.

Subalpine Parkland

The parklike mosaic of meadows and groups of trees with many colorful flowers looks like it has been there a long time, and it has. It is easy to think of it as permanent, though we do notice many small changes when we go back to a spot we have visited some years previously. On a larger time scale, many of the meadows are slowly evolving into forests; we can see that small trees are establishing themselves. Because they grow so slowly they are often much older than they look. Approximate estimates of age can be made by counting the rows of branches.

Younger trees are often seen growing around the older ones. In addition, in many of the lower meadows a large number of young trees of approximately the same age are growing throughout. This invasion has been found to have taken place during a slightly warmer and drier climatic period between about 1910 and 1940, at about the same time that many of the glaciers in this area receded remarkably. Less snow meant the meadows melted free earlier in the summer, thus giving the seedlings their start. Some of these seedlings may be seen in the lower meadows of Spray Park.

The flowery meadows at various elevations often have developed as a result of wildfire sometime during the past several hundred years. Look for stumps, logs, and other evidence of a previous forest.

On the big volcanic peaks and some of the other high mountains, trees are possibly still advancing upward, not yet having had enough time since Ice Age glaciation to reach as high as they eventually may. Trees move upward only one short step at a time, as far away as their seeds can be dispersed. If a seed germinates and the tree lives to maturity, this tree's seeds move one more step.

Mixture of red and white heather photographed in the upper meadows of Spray Park, Mount Rainier. Taken in mid-July with a 35mm Canon camera on Kodachrome II film. Subalpine fir in center background; mountain hemlock on the right.

Heather

Though both are commonly called heather, the low shrubs pictured on pages 112-113 represent two genera in the heath family: The white one is *Cassiope mertensiana*, the red one, *Phyllodoce empetriformis*.

These heathers are common around timberline, a rather broad term given to that part of a mountain where trees become smaller and scattered. On cool, north slopes particularly, the heathers may form a rather stable community apparently in balance with its environment. The coolness, which we notice as a difference in temperature when we walk the slopes in summer, has a more important effect on the plants in another way. Remember how in winter the shady side of the street always keeps the snow longer, and sometimes it does not completely melt before more snow falls, while the sunny side may have melted clear several times? The same thing happens on a mountain, though on a much bigger scale, and sunny south slopes will be free of snow before the cooler north sides, if other things such as the actual amount of precipitation are equal. And where snow remains on the ground so long as to make the growing season extremely short, only certain plants are able to become established. Heather can do it with a growing season that is just slightly shorter than what trees require. Apparently, white and red heather are fairly equal in these and other requirements, since we so often see them growing together.

The forbs, as the flowers with non-woody stems are called, can grow where the season is shorter. It may be that the season is shorter because snow melts late, so we see them blooming in what appears to us a moist site. Or, the growing season may be short because the site dries out later in the summer, so we think of it as a dry situation; in this case we see the flowers bloom earlier. The actual growing season may be much the same in either case.

Left, White Heather (Cassiope mertensiana). Above, Red Heather (Phyllodoce empetriformis)

White Heather

Cassiope *mertensiana* (Heath Family)

White heather is an abundant low shrub, like the red heather found near timberline and requiring well-drained soil yet plenty of moisture. Its pure white nodding bells grow singly on little stalks rising from the axils of the leaves. The leaves are scale-like, closely pressed against the branches, with appear four-angled.

Red, yellow, and white heathers may be found growing together, particularly on top of minor Cascade peaks. On larger mountains with a wider elevation span of heather slopes, red heather is lowest, white heather comes in a little higher, and yellow heather at highest elevations, usually above timberline. Yellow heather also grows farthest northward. Though the red seems a bit more common in the Cascades, white heather has the wider distribution along the Pacific Coast. It is found farther south, down in the Sierras, where the red is represented by a different species.

White heather is said to have been John Muir's favorite flower, except that being a Scotsman, he used the name cassiope, rather than confuse it with the common or Scotch heather, *Calluna vulgaris,* found in Europe. Gardners commonly lump together as heathers the cultivated forms of both *Calluna* and *Erica,* another genus native in the Old World but not in America. An attempt to save the name heather for *Calluna,* and use the name heath for the *Ericas,* is a battle that appears to have been lost in English as it is written and spoken throughout the world. There is, then, little hope for a minor cause, along the same lines of thinking, that would assign mountain heather to *Cassiope* and mountain heath to *Phyllodoce,* because of similarity of leaf structure to the corresponding British plant. Blossom forms are quite different.

The rather similar, also white-flowered, *Cassiope tetragona,* is the widespread heather of the Arctic.

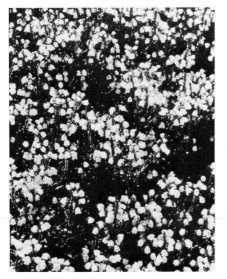

Photographed at Spray Park, Mount Rainier, in mid-July with a 35mm Canon camera on High Speed Ektachrome.

118

Red Heather
Phyllodoce empetriformis (Heath Family)

Red (or pink) heather is one of the common shrubs growing around timberline in Northwest mountains, very attractive during its short season of bloom. It is found particularly on ridges and steep slopes; if growing in a moist meadow, it will often snuggle against and grow over a big rock. A low shrub, protected by snow during the winter, it begins to flower within a few weeks after it is uncovered. Evergreen needle-like leaves grow thickly around the branches which are topped by a cluster of rosy bells; the small red seedpods topping the stems serve to identify the plant after the flowers are gone. Flowers are about the same size as those of the white heather—the red plant was photographed from a closer distance.

The yellow heather, *Phyllodoce glanduliflora,* has similar leaves and a few greenish-yellow closed-bell flowers. It reaches more alpine heights than does the red.

In boggy spots beside mountain pools there is a small pink-flowered shrub sometimes mistaken for heather, the kalmia. Instead of nodding bells it has saucer-shaped flowers facing upwards. Not as abundant as heather, it is most common on the north side of Mount Rainier, as in Spray and Seattle Parks; it is also seen in places like Lyman Lake and Table Mountain.

A deep, soft carpet that looks a little like heather and has round black berries is crowberry. This far-northern plant, whose fruit is relished by Eskimos, also grows at high elevations. The juice is refreshing on a hot day if you spit out the somewhat bitter seeds and skin. Nineteenth century European botanists saw the resemblance in the opposite direction and named our red heather after the crowberry, *Empetrum nigrum.*

Photographed along the Golden Gate trail in Paradise Valley, Mount Rainier National Park.

Above, Green Hellebore (Veratrum viride). Right, White Hellebore (Veratrum californicum)

Columbine (Aquilegia formosa)

Meadow Parsley

Ligusticum grayi **(Parsley Family)**

Lupine meadows usually contain quite an admixture of frothy white, an effect provided by several kinds of plants with many tiny flowers on top of a slender stem. One of these is *Ligusticum grayi*, locally called meadow parsley. Like other members of the family, its flowers are arranged in an umbel, all the flowerstalks arising from one point on the stem and forming a flat-topped cluster (for a bottom view of this form, see the photograph of cow parsnip, p. 108). Actually, this is a compound umbel, each stalk bearing a smaller or secondary umbel. The plant keeps on producing flowers for a long time, and after most surrounding flowers have faded there may still be a few blossom heads on the meadow parsley.

Other white flowers commonly found with lupine are the bistort (pictured on p. 176) and the Sitka valerian. The valerian has a humped flower cluster; though all near the top of the stem, the flowerstalks arise in opposite pairs, one above the other, in a branched arrangement. Its buds are pale pink.

This meadow parsley grows from the Cascades of Washington to the Sierras of California, east through the Blue Mountain region of northeastern Oregon to central Idaho. Its leaves are mainly basal, long-stemmed and much dissected. *Ligusticum canbyi* is a much larger plant with more leafy stems, also found in the Wenatchee and Cascade Mountains of central and northern Washington.

The plant pictured is sometimes called Gray's ligusticum, or Gray's lovage, lovage being the English name for a European species of *Ligusticum*. In the past ours was listed as *L. purpureum*.

Both photographs taken in July on the Naches Peak trail near Chinook Pass, with 35mm Canon camera on High Speed Ektachrome film. Dewey Lake in the distance.

Columbine   *Aquilegia formosa* (Buttercup Family)

This, the only columbine in the Cascades, is reminiscent of the red columbine found in eastern America, except that the flower is more open. This species is found in open areas from the lowlands up to the subalpine zone, not everywhere, but a damp cliff or a meadow are likely spots.

The elaborate structure of the columbine flower, as is the case with other members of the buttercup family, includes some parts that are not what they appear. Flaring outward are the bright red sepals. Yellow petals are comparatively short and point downward; attached to them is a tall red spur which contains nectar in the terminal knob. (In some botanical descriptions you may read the spurs are at the "base" of the petals—this is botanical talk for the end attached to the plant).

The bright red flower attracts not bees—they are blind to this color—but hummingbirds, who have learned to associate with food any shade from deep pink of early-flowering currant to this scarlet, found also in some of the paintbrushes and the scarlet gilia, to orange as the honeysuckle. All contain nectar at the end of long tubes, mutually adapted to the hummingbirds with their long bills and tongues. As the bird hovers below the columbine, its breast or head is dusted with pollen, which he carries along when he flits to the next one. Hummingbird flowers have little need for fragrance as the birds do not have a highly-developed sense of smell; they depend on the flash of color. Both rufous and the tiny calliope hummingbirds are frequent in mountain meadows and will often buzz a red jacket or scarf.

Photographed in July near Owyhigh Lakes, Mount Rainier National Park, with a 35mm camera with a 200mm lens at ground level. Also may be seen on Chinook Pass and below the highway near Paradise Inn.

Rosy Spirea (Spirea densiflora)

White Rhododendron (Rhododendron albiflorum)

The soft fuzzy effect comes from the numerous long stamens; actually the filaments (the stalk part of the stamens), which in many flowers are almost colorless, are conspicuous in this flower because they are both elongated and colored pink like the petals. Pollen, borne on the tiny knob (the anther) at the end of the stamens, is out where no insect could possible miss being brushed by it.

Rosy spirea is a shrub 2 or 3 feet tall, growing in subalpine meadows of western mountains.

Flowers very like these, except for the shape of the cluster, are found on the closely-related steeplebush, *Spirea douglasii*, with fingerlike spikes of the same fuzzy pink. A taller shrub, growing at lower elevations, it is also called hardhack, and its branches were used by Lummi Indians for spreading and cooking salmon. There is a white spirea, too, knee-high or less, that is more common on the east slope of the Cascades; its blossom clusters are flat. Other relatives, which in common with the spireas have small flowers gathered together in showy blossom clusters, are the luetkea (pictured on page 192) and the ocean spray.

Ocean spray (*Holodiscus discolor*) is the biggest of these shrubs, 6 or 8 feet tall. Foamy flower panicles, cream in color, appear about the same time as fireweed. Branches are straight and tough. The wood was used by Western Washington Indians for many tools: roasting tongs, digging sticks for clams and roots, duck or flounder spears; in other areas, for arrow shafts.

Rosy spirea growing against a boulder on the trail to Van Trump Park, Mount Rainer, taken in early August with a 35mm Canon camera on High Speed Ektachrome film.

White Rhododendron   *Rhododendron albiflorum* (Heath Family)

Flowers are along the stem instead of terminal as in most rhododendrons, but the cluster of leaves at the end of the stem is comfortably rhododendron-like. The leaves have a shiny look, easily distinguished from those of menziesia. White rhododendron grows on wet mountain slopes from British Columbia to Oregon, east to the northern Rockies, generally in open spots in the upper forest. It is a deciduous shrub, 4 or 5 feet tall, developing fairly late in the season, though buds are made the previous year. Large thickets may be formed. The slender, resilient branches are deceptively easy to walk on when still bent to the ground from the weight of winter snow, but are some of the most slippery, the light-colored bark slipping off easily and exposing the yellow, wet inner layer.

The pink-flowered, evergreen *Rhododendron macrophyllum,* which is Washington's state flower, skips the Washington Cascades. It is coastal from British Columbia through Washington and moves into the Cascades in Oregon; it also grows in northern California. Members of the heath family usually inhabit acid soils, such as those found in forests. Also, generally, wet or moist soils or a moist climate, so there are many of them in the mountains and the northern forests. Comparatively, though, the pink one grows in drier places than the white rhododendron.

"Albiflorum" means white-flowered. This shrub is also called Cascades azalea, azalea being a popular name for deciduous rhododendrons. (It grows in the Olympics and Rockies, too.)

Photographed above Thornton Lakes in the North Cascades National Park. Taken with a 4x5-inch Super Graphic. This shrub is abundant along the Cascade Crest Trail in the Porcupine Creek valley a few miles north of Rainy Pass.

131

Timberline Trees

The Cascades are influenced by a maritime climate with a lot of winter precipitation which falls as snow in the mountains, more on the west side than the east. One of the causes of timberline is a snowpack that lies so long on the ground that the growing season is not long enough for trees to become established, though from an historic standpoint trees sometimes have not had time enough to get as high as they may eventually go. (Mount St. Helens, particularly, because it is a young volcano, has a low apparent timberline and its highest trees are not typical timberline species.)

Mountain hemlock and subalpine fir are probably the most common timberline trees in the Cascades. Most of the trees in this photograph are subalpine fir, while both may be seen in the picture of heather, mountain hemlock on the right, subalpine fir in the center (p. 112). Because growth is slow, these short trees at timberline may be surprisingly old. Though gnarled and twisted when they grow here, just a little lower the same species exhibit a spirelike form.

The subalpine fir and the mountain hemlock can take the 50- to 80-foot annual snowfall, as at Paradise. Twenty or 30 feet may be on the ground at once. The little trees are flattened in winter and trunks may acquire permanent bends, but they survive. Pacific silver fir, much more subject to breakage because of its rigidity, grows in the protection of other trees, as does the Alaska cedar. Whitebark pine may be a scrub tree at high elevations. When branches of certain species are buried in snow too long, a fungus causes the needles to turn black and die.

On the east side Engelmann spruce is also prominent. The Lyall larch grows at timberline in the North Cascades; this is a tree with rather limited range found only from here east to southwestern Alberta and western Montana.

Mount Rainier rising over a field of paintbrush in Spray Park, on the north side of the mountain, photographed at the end of July, with a 35mm Canon camera on Kodachrome II.

Paintbrushes come in many shades from whitish, light to golden yellow, orange to scarlet, and faded old rose to crimson and magenta, as well as slightly brownish or purplish. Bright ones attract the most attention. Most of the color is in the bracts, the leafy appendages under each individual flower on the stalk. Often the tube-shaped calyxes have colored tips, while the flower itself is quite hidden and inconspicuous. Paintbrushes are partially parasitic on other plants. There seems to be reason to suspect that their abundance varies from year to year. On return visits to meadows where paintbrush has been very showy, it is sometimes much less in evidence.

Botanists admit this is a difficult genus. Though some help in identifying species, color cannot be depended upon entirely; in fact, one of the things to enjoy about paintbrushes is their many hues. The amount of hairiness is not particularly reliable either, but should be noticed. Habitat is another clue, helpful at times, but apt to change with the climate; for example, *C. miniata* at Mount Rainier is seen usually on steep and dry sunny slopes, while in areas like the Wenatchee Mountains of Lake Chelan, it grows in streamside habitats. Whether leaves and/or bracts have lobes, whether these are blunt or pointed, and the shape of the calyx lobes and corollas, are important distinguishing characters. It helps to sketch these parts in the field and check them with an illustrated technical manual. It does not help to find out that there is quite a bit of variation, suspected to be due to hybridization.

The scientific name honors Spanish botanist Domingo Castillejo, the first species described having come from Colombia. The species pictured is probably *C. parviflora* var. *oreopola*, the common meadow species at Mount Rainer, and usually a more magenta-pink shade. The flowers are a little shorter than some of the other kinds, resulting in a narrower "brush."

Above, White Paintbrush (Castilleja parviflora var. albida). Right, Magenta Paintbrush (Castilleja parviflora var. oreopola)

The two photographs on the preceding pages are of the same species of paintbrush, but different varieties, one the magenta-pink paintbrush common at Mount Rainier, the other found only in the North Cascades. The northern variety, common in high meadows, is pale-colored, slightly pinkish or brownish, greenish-white or greenish-yellow. (Around Harts Pass and perhaps other places there is a rose-colored form, because of matching flower size still included by botanists with var. *albida,* rather than with the darker Mount Rainier variety.)

Colors are of help in telling paintbrush species apart only when accompanied by careful attention to shapes of leaves, bracts, and flowers. A widespread species, usually a scarlet or orange-red, is *C. miniata,* with short, sharp-pointed lobes on the bracts and entire (unlobed) leaves. Bracts and flowers are longer than *C. parviflora* and spread outward more. On the east side of the Cascades it may be either a bright crimson or a soft old-rose shade, with a branching stem. Also frequent, but scattered, is the round-lobed *C. hispida,* with yellow, orange, or red bracts. Bright red *C. elmeri* with sticky hairs grows only on the east side. Found only at high altitudes, on cliffs and rocky ridges, is *C. rupicola,* a very short plant with brilliant scarlet bracts and dark red leaves, both divided into long, narrow, blunt lobes. It grows with such plants as the golden fleabane and the miniature Lyall lupine, and may be seen high in Spray Park and on Burroughs Mountain at Mount Rainier, or in the North Cascades.

White paintbrush photographed in late July on top of Excelsior Mountain near Mount Baker, with a 4x5-inch Super Graphic. Taken a few minutes after a dense fog had lifted, leaving everything covered with a fine dew.

Magenta Paintbrush   *Castilleja parviflora var. oreopola* (Figwort Family)

This photograph exhibits some of the problems in naming paintbrush species. The color and form which struck the photographer make for chancy identification. Bracts with a blunt-tipped center lobe and long narrow spreading ones on the side are those of the variety given above. It should have lobes on the leaves to conform completely, and the crimson-pink color is unusual, too. A deep magenta-pink shade (not too successfully reproduced on film and less so in print) is the one more commonly seen in this variety, which grows only in the Cascades from the Mount Rainier area to the Three Sisters in Oregon. A very similar pink paintbrush grows in meadows in the Olympics (*C. parviflora* var. *olympica*). In the North Cascades, south as far as the vicinity of Stevens Pass, is found the other variety (var. *albida*), usually whitish, while the area of Snoqualmie Pass and most of the proposed Alpine Lakes Wilderness Area appears to be without either the white or the pink one. This is an interesting "unoccupied zone" for which there is as yet no explanation; many other plants range right through.

All three varieties are plants of subalpine and alpine meadows, common in their respective ranges. They are easy (?) to distinguish from other kinds growing in our area, which are generally in the orange to red spectrum, by the hairy leaves and bracts with one of two pair of long narrow lateral lobes—check the leaf shape in the closeup photograph of the white one. Or, perhaps it would be better to suggest that persons interested in paintbrushes spend a few seasons just looking; when they seem to settle down to only four or five general types, start trying to identify them.

The variety pictured has also been listed separately as *Castilleja oreopola*. The average person might ignore varietal names if not interested in the color differences. "Parviflora" means small-flowered, a fairly appropriate designation, since the flowers are a little shorter than in our other species.

Photographed at Chinook Pass in mid-July with a 35mm Canon camera on Kodachrome II film.

139

Meadow flowers and Sloan Peak

Jacob's Ladder (Polemonium pulcherrimum)

Lupine (Lupinus latifolia var. subalpinus)

Meadow Flagers

View of Sloan Peak and flowers growing above White Pass (Glacier Peak Wilderness Area). Taken with a 35mm Canon camera using a 200mm lens to make Sloan Peak stand out and High Speed Ektachrome film to bring the flowers into focus in spite of a light wind.

While shots portraying a single flower are more practical for an introductory book, it should be understood that these flowers do not often grow alone. Each mountain meadow is a mixture of many plants, and there is endless variety of form and color. Here we have blue (lupine), lavender (mountain daisy or fleabane) and white (bistort not quite in full bloom), photographed in late July.

Jacob's Ladder; Polemonium

Polemonium pulcherrimum (Phlox Family)

Jacob's ladder photographed near Sunrise parking lot, Mount Rainier, in mid-July, with a 35mm Canon camera on High Speed Ektachrome film.

These are leafy plants up to a foot tall which often grow around the edges of clumps of trees in subalpine meadows. The sky-blue flowers usually have a yellow center—the tube part of the flower; as is typical of the phlox family, there is a long narrow tube with five spreading lobes.

The leaflets are supposed to represent rungs on a ladder. Jacob's ladder is a traditional name used for various species of polemonium, particularly tall ones; the generic name is also used. Leaves of most polemoniums have more or less of an odor of skunk—don't step on them!

Several other polemoniums are found in the Cascades, one a smaller variety of this species. Another is the most attractive *P. elegans*, a high alpine which forms a low cushion of thickly-crowded leaflets and has large purple flowers. The plant pictured, *P. pulcherrimum* var. *calycinum* to be very exact, has also been listed under *P. columbianum* and several other names.

Lupine

Lupinus latifolia var. subalpinus (Pea Family)

From seashores to mountaintops, from the plains of Texas, where they are affectionately known as bluebonnets, to the Arctic near timberline, and also in the Mediterranean area, grow many kinds of lupine. They are members of the pea family, as evidenced by the individual flowers and the seedpods. Their leaves, however, have a distinctive pattern—each with many finger-like leaflets radiating from a central point, a particularly artistic design when holding a sparkling drop of dew or rainwater. Most have blue flowers, but a few of the shore kinds are yellow. Fairly often, plants with pure white flowers may be found among the blue; rarely, one with pink blossoms—in either of these cases it is a color form, not a different species.

The lupine pictured is the glory of Cascade meadows, forming big fields of blue, often mixed with white of mountain dock, valerian, and parsley. There may be accents of yellow from arnicas and senecios, pink or reds of various paintbrushes, or lavender mountain daisies. At times, when the air is warm and still, when the flower's stage of development is just right, there is a wonderful fragrance, reminiscent of sweet peas. Lupine seeds at certain stages are poisonous, but marmots seem to enjoy the flowers. Dying back to the ground each fall, lupine is ready to bloom by the midpoint of the flowering season, but depending upon when the snow has melted off a particular spot can be seen from late July to late September.

It may be called subalpine lupine to distinguish it from other species, and is sometimes listed under _L. subalpinus._ The former _L. volcanicus_ is now considered the same variety.

Photographed on Panorama Point, Mount Rainier, in early August, with a 35mm Canon camera on High Speed Ektachrome film. Lupine fields on the slopes of Alta Vista are outstanding; Meadow Mountain east of Darrington is another good place.

Cascade Crest Trail crossing meadow in Glacier Peak Wilderness Area

Mountain Ash (Sorbus scopulina)

A circumboreal plant rather scattered in distribution in the Northwest: in open grassy places and often on rocky ridges, from sealevel to 6000 feet. Though seen blooming on the gravelly Tacoma prairies (glacial outwash left from the Ice Age) in June and photographed here at a moderate elevation on the east side of the Cascades in July, at fairly high altitudes in the mountains bluebell is typically a late-blooming flower.

Doubtless there are many places where it grows in quantity, but two which linger in memory are the top of Tolmie Peak and the Moraine Park trail beside the Carbon Glacier in Mount Rainier National Park. The bells are huge. The plants are growing in spots where they receive a lot of sun, possibly a requirement. Places warm and dry and sunny enough to be grassy also are likely to be right for bluebells, though not if the sod gets too thick. This may be why bluebells are backed up against the wall, so to speak, in the rocky places. There may be certain soil requirements, also, which would help to explain distribution of bluebells in mountains. Size of the flower varies a lot; those pictured are large ones. More typical ones are only about a ½-inch wide.

Bluebell is a name people like to use. This one is called bluebell of Scotland to distinguish it from the English bluebell in the lily family, from Virginia bluebell and others among the mertensias. Campanula means "little bell." Though no more (nor less) associated with mountains than this flower, western mertensias are sometimes called mountain bluebells. Under these circumstances it is well to learn two names in order to explain which bluebell you are talking about. "Rotundifolia" refers to a few round leaves at the base of the plant, which are often withered by flowering time, making people wonder how that name ever came to be given.

Photographed near Fish Lake in the Cle Elum valley in mid-July; with a 35mm Canon camera on High Speed Ektachrome film.

Arnica and Trail Scene

One of the arnicas is prominent in this picture, *A. latifolia,* an important species in mountain meadows. It also grows with the heathers. Flowers are yellow; leaves opposite each other on the stem distinguish it from senecios. Telling it from several other arnicas growing in the Cascades is a bit more difficult. They are in the composite family.

Meadow flowers lining a narrow path are a sign that the trail is not heavily used; the flowers do not stand much trampling. Where erosion of the soil by water running down the trail is not a problem, meadow vegetation may grow into an unbeaten path, though not as aggressively as does the brush at lower elevations where the growing season is longer.

Cascade Crest Trail around the side of Indian Head Peak, going toward White Pass, Glacier Peak Wilderness Area; taken in July with 35mm Canon camera on High Speed Ektachrome film.

Mountain Ash   Sorbus scopulina (Rose Family)

Two species of mountain ash grow in Northwest mountains, this one with pointed leaflets, dark green and glossy. Its bright red berries are also glossy. Hikers covering a good deal of the Cascades are apt to see more of the *Sorbus sitchensis* variety which has leaflets rounded at the outer end and a dull grayish green (var. *grayi*). Both are shrubs around 3 to 5 feet tall, growing at forest edges. The photograph was taken at Sunrise on Mount Rainier, where both kinds have been included in the plantings around the visitor center and restrooms. This is a good place to learn the difference between them as they are not otherwise likely to be seen together. One variety of the species pictured has been called *S. cascadensis.*

Taken in mid-July with 35mm Canon camera on High Speed Ektachrome. There is a whole hillside of mountain ash above Trapper Lake in the North Cascades.

Left, Thistle (Cirsium edule). Above, Pinguicula or Butterwort (Pinguicula vulgaris)

Spiderweb-like wool around the buds and spiny involucre (the bracts enclosing the base of the flower head) dresses up this thistle and sets it apart from introduced kinds. It is called the edible thistle, and one wonders why, as it does not have an appetizing look (except to the bumblebee searching for nectar). This name is a translation of the scientific one given to the plant by Harvard professor Thomas Nuttall, who described it after he had made a trip to the West Coast in 1834-1836 with Nathaniel Wyeth, Boston fur trader. He mentioned that Indians peeled the thick, succulent stems and ate them. Whether this is the same species eaten during the Oregon winter of the Lewis and Clark expedition, described by Meriwether Lewis as a 9- to 15-inch-long thistle root, very sweet when baked by the Indian method, is uncertain. Oregon and Plains Indians, but not those of Western Washington, apparently made use of several kinds of thistle in these ways. In lower elevations in the Northwest, *C. brevistylum* also has succulent, edible stems. Its styles (stigma-bearing stalks), however, never extend much beyond the tiny flower lobes, while those of *C. edule* are exerted, extending well beyond the corollas. *Cirsium edule* is the thistle found in mountain meadows of the Cascades; here it does not grow as large as in parts of its range.

Thistles have a type of composite head which has only disk flowers—narrow tubular ones each containing style and stamens. The tiny flowers packed closely together inside the involucre offer an insect-attracting splash of color en masse.

Taken in early September in Horseshoe Basin up the Stehekin valley, with a 35mm Canon camera on High Speed Ektachrome. Thistles seem to be a favorite food supply for bees. Put your camera on a tripod and use a long cable release, wait a few moments and a bee is sure to come along.

Pinguicula; Butterwort

Pinguicula vulgaris (Bladderwort Family)

On first sight it looks like a violet; at second glance it is obviously something else. Yellow-green leaves, growing flat against the ground, have a greasy look, hence the old English name, butterwort. The leaves secrete a glue-like substance which traps small insects, and a digestive enzyme which breaks down their softer parts to be absorbed, leaving skeleton remains. Outer edges of the leaves may fold in on the insects to hasten the digestive process. The plant pictured has had a banquet; though it is usual to see a few dead insects in any patch of pinguicula, this many is extraordinary. The flower stems are 2 to 4 inches tall, occasionally more; leaves are up to an inch wide. This, the common pinguicula, is a circumboreal plant (found completely around the northern hemisphere). In the Northwest it grows in the mountains, in wet mossy banks and dripping rock crevices.

The family is named after the bladderworts, aquatic plants with submerged leaves, growing in standing or slowly-moving water, ponds, ditches, and such, and using small bladders with one-way valves to trap minute water animals. They are not particularly to be expected in the mountains. The family is a small one, best-developed in the tropics.

Another carnivorous plant is the tiny sundew (in the sundew family), which has sticky, gland-tipped red stalks on its leaves. Insects are trapped by the stickiness and adjacent stalks then curve over to hold them down against the leaf which, excluding the long petiole, is about the size of a fingernail. The sundew is also a circumboreal plant, found in sphagnum bogs or sometimes on a waterlogged rotten log at the edge of a lake, occasionally in such places in the mountains. None of the well-known pitcher-plant family are native in Washington. Insectivorous plants are usually found in boggy places where there may be a deficiency of available nutrients, particularly nitrogen.

Pinguicula taken the first of August near Comet Falls on the trail to Van Trump Park, Mount Rainier; found on a shaded damp hillside. Photographed with a 35mm Canon camera on High Speed Ektachrome. Also seen on the old trail to Cascade Pass, near White Rock Lakes, near the DeRoux Campground on the Teanaway River road, near Washington Pass, and in other places.

Only one pink mimulus is found along Northwest mountain streams, so species identification is easy. It was named after Meriwether Lewis, who collected it while crossing the Rockies; the name Lewis monkeyflower serves to distinguish it from such monkeyflowers in other areas as the pink-flowered desert annuals, one of which appears in dry pumice in the southern Oregon Cascades.

Most species of mimulus are water-loving plants; this one will be found lining mountain streams. The plant is one or two feet tall, often forming large clumps. Flowers are about 1½ inches long, their color variously described as red, pink, purple, rose-red, or magenta, with two yellow patches marking the throat. They bloom fairly late in the season and when finished the corollas drop into the water to keep fresh and colorful for some days longer. Green, mossy patches often associated with the monkeyflowers include both mosses and leafy liverworts; in the picture some scattered yellow mimulus may be seen in the moss. If it grew intermixed, the shorter yellow species would be hidden under the thick foliage of the pink one; instead, it grows along the edge nearer the water.

(Top) Pink mimulus photographed along the Naches Peak trail near Chinook Pass, with 35mm Canon camera on High Speed Ektachrome film.

(Bottom) Taken along the Paradise River near the trail to the Ice Caves, with 35mm Canon camera, High Speed Ektachrome. This is a well-known mimulus paradise; mimulus is also memorable in Horseshoe Basin in the upper Stehekin.

Either monkeyflower or mimulus are used as common names for these plants, as the user chooses. To specify the one pictured on page 160 it is clearest to use Lewis, but people who may be concerned only about distinguishing the color may prefer to say pink.

Monkeyflowers are members of the figwort family, related to foxgloves, snapdragons, paintbrushes, pedicularis, and penstemons. Penstemons, whose tubular flowers have very small lobes, so that the tubes rather than faces are the conspicuous part of the flower, are typical of rock outcrops, dry cliffs and ridges, instead of moist streambanks. They tend to lavender and blue-purple shades and generally bloom earlier than the mimulus.

Among the penstemons are several dwarf, mat-forming shrubs. The most common in the Washington Cascades is Davidson's penstemon (*P. davidsonii*), with rounded, evergreen, leathery leaves and inch-long lavender flowers. At somewhat lower elevations grows the similar shrubby penstemon (*P. fruticosus*) whose leaves have an acute tip. Bright rose flowers contrasted with gray leaves mark the cliff penstemon, *P. rupicola*. Rock outcrops and dry cliffs where these shrub penstemons live are particularly rugged environments. Rainwater quickly disappears and there are long periods of drought. In some sites snow may not stick to form a protective covering against winter wind and cold, as it does over the subalpine meadows. A waxy covering on the leaves helps to retard water loss in both these periods. The mats get a start in cracks in the rock, which become filled with windborne and fallen materials, dust, sand, and organic, resulting also in an increase of waterholding capacity. Mat-forming plants are especially well-suited to intercept and hold more materials, thus building the soil outward from the crack.

Pink mimulus photographed on a very wet hillside with continuous surface seepage, in Seattle Park on the north side of Mount Rainier. Taken in mid-July with 4x5-inch Super Graphic camera.

Beargrass (Xerophyllum tenax)

Ptarmigan hen

Beargrass

Tales about beargrass are many, but exact information which would explain its erratic bloom appears to be scant. One year there is quite a lot, in others, not much. It is certain that it takes some years for a beargrass plant to become large enough to send up a blooming stalk; it is also said that the rhizome produces offshoot plants which develop for several years before blooming, after which that particular offshoot dies. In the meantime other offshoots are in the process of development. Few blossoms are seen in patches growing in the forest, and beargrass is known to become luxuriant after a fire or logging, apparently responding to the additional light. This might account for certain showy displays developing at a particular time, and plants in that patch might be in lock step afterward. But this does not explain why other beargrass should be in step, too, if it is really true that there are "good beargrass years." There could be some correlation with weather during certain past growing seasons. It is true of mountain flowering in general that weather during the previous growing season makes a difference, since most plants develop buds or stored energy the year before the flower appears. The question is, what sort of a season presages a good beargrass year when?

Beargrass is common in the northern Rockies of the United States and also in mountains of the Northwest, in open areas in the upper forest. Its scientific name means dry-leaved and tough. The grass-like leaves, which grow in a big tuft, were used by Indian women in making baskets, and for decorative designs by the coastal people who made their basic baskets of red cedarbark or spruce roots. On a steep slope they are slippery underfoot. Unlike most herbage in subalpine meadows which dies down in the winter, these leaves remain green. Though too tough for the taste of most larger grazing or browsing mammals except the mountain goat, they are eaten by the large meadow vole and included in the haypile of the pika. Tender flower buds are nipped off by the larger animals, however.

Photographed in late July near Paradise Inn at Mount Rainier, with 35mm Canon camera on High Speed Ektachrome film. There are large fields on the Bench Lake trail, Mount Rainier; on Huckleberry Mountain near Enumclaw; and in Blankenship Meadows on the Cascade Crest Trail south of Rainier.

Ptarmigan and Pussytoes

Ptarmigan are seen near or above timberline, in heather or sparsely-vegetated areas. They rely on speckled camouflage to hide from predators, the fluffy chicks freezing where they are and their mother moving off some distance to decoy the invader away from them. This makes it difficult to do a family portrait. They have been observed eating flowers of heather and mountain dock, leaves of *Eriogonum pyrolaefolium*, seeds of Tolmie saxifrage, and diet in general includes seeds, buds (particularly of heather), berries, insects.

Other common residents of alpine areas are the small rosy finches who travel in flocks and may be seen over snowfields and glaciers hunting frozen and benumbed insects. Also seedeaters, they nest in alpine cliffs. Each plant and animal has its own particular habitat where it finds what it needs to live. Mountain communities are sorted by altitude level, climatic conditions being progressively more severe in higher zones. The alpine zone is the area above timberline; it is found only on the higher peaks in Washington, mostly snow, ice, and rock, with only small areas or narrow bands on which vegetation is developed.

Pussytoes (*Antennaria* species) are members of the composite family, with staminate and pistillate flowers on separate plants, sometimes setting seed without fertilization. Several have white-woolly leaves and may cover the ground in patches which can be seen from a distance, while the flowers are rather inconspicuous. The closely-packed flower heads with their dark outlines are supposed to look like the underside of a cat's foot. (Pussypaws, on the other hand, have a fluffy flower reminiscent of the furry top view.)

Ptarmigan hen photographed on White Pass near Glacier Peak. Taken in late July with 35mm camera using 200mm lens.

Above, Tweedy's Lewisia, (Lewisia tweedyi).

Below, Columbia Lewisia (Lewisia columbiana). Right, Elephanthead (Pedicularis groenlandica)

Tweedy's Lewisia

Lewisia tweedyi (Purslane Family)

The 2- or 3-inch flowers are often darker than these pictured, in blended shades of apricot and peach not found in any other wildflower. Tweedy's lewisia grows in the Wenatchee Mountains area, mainly in the ponderosa pine zone, on well-drained rocky slopes. Tumwater Canyon Botanical Area northwest of Leavenworth is a good place to see it. Frank Tweedy was the man who collected it while a member of a survey team working out the route of the Northern Pacific Railway.

This is the largest of the lewisias, a group of plants with thick, fleshy roots, named after Meriwether Lewis of the Lewis and Clark Expedition. The best-known is the bitterroot, Montana's state flower and after

which the Bitterroot Mountains were named; it was extensively dug by the Indians and was one of the plants brought back by the Expedition. One of their purposes being to gather information about the natural resources of the area, the Lewis and Clark team collected specimens of other plants with edible roots or bulbs including camas, several lomatiums, spring beauty, glacier lily, balsamroot; berries such as salal, salmonberry, Oregon grape, evergreen huckleberry; and ocean spray whose branches were used for arrows. They first described in detail the grizzly bear, pronghorn, mule, and Columbia black-tailed deer, mountain goat, mountain beaver, and prairie dog. Two birds were named after them, the Lewis woodpecker and Clark's nutcracker. The latter has recently been discovered to be influential in the spread of whitebark pine in timberline areas, as this bird makes seed caches which sometimes are not eaten. Several other plants commemorate their names: clarkia; the syringia, *Philadelphus lewisii*, which became Idaho's state flower; and the Lewis mimulus. Other flowers pictured in this book, brought back by them, are trillium, scarlet gilia, and bistort.

Tweedy's lewisia was photographed on a cloudy day in late May, in Swakane Canyon near Wenatchee. Taken with 4x5-inch Super Graphic.

Columbia Lewisia

Lewisia columbiana (Purslane Family)

Columbia lewisia has much smaller flowers, about as big as your little fingernail, in an open branching raceme 6 inches tall. Their seven to nine petals distinguish them from several related plants of similar size, the spring beauty and miner's lettuce species (*Montia*), which have five petals. The thick root is another distinction, very obvious from the shape of the crown from which grow the

strap-shaped succulent leaves. Found on dry, rocky outcrops from southern British Columbia to California; in the Cascades, mainly on the east side.

Photographed close to the top of Mount David near Lake Wenatchee, in late August, using a 35mm Canon camera and High Speed Ektachrome film.

170

Elephanthead   *Pedicularis groenlandica* (Figwort Family)

From Labrador to the Sierra Nevada these perfect little red elephants may be found decorating tall flower spikes above fern-like leaves. Generally in a wet habitat, such as streamsides and small depressions; apparently always in such spots in the Cascades though in some other places it is part of ordinary alpine meadow vegetation. Here it is usually found in the subalpine zone, in open sunny areas, not shady spots. Six to 12 inches tall, its leaves are similar to those of the yellow pedicularis following. The "trunk" is an extension of the upper lip of the flower, technically referred to as a beak. As might be expected of such a widespread flower, the elephanthead varies slightly according to geographic area and these differences have been recognized by some botanists as separate varieties. *Pedicularis surrecta* is a synonym under which ours may be listed.

Photographed in Glacier Basin, Mount Rainier, in mid-July, with a 4x5-inch Super Graphic camera.

The person who cannot go to far places to get acquainted with plant life which might be compared with that of our mountains can nevertheless acquire a feel of similarities and differences through the armchair method. In addition to the obvious books on mountain life, some popular yet meaty writings that will interest flower lovers: In *Reading the Landscape,* by May T. Watts (Macmillan), a chapter on alpine plant life, its various adaptations for coping with cold, with drought, with a short growing season, particularly in the Rockies. *The Voice of the Desert,* by Joseph W. Krutch (Sloane), for devices for economizing water; when there is little rain in summer, cliffs, scree, and pumice fields are rather like a desert, including hot daytime temperatures. *Arctic Year,* by Peter Freuchen and Finn Salomonsen (Putnam's), an insight into conditions in which plants live in the Arctic, some of the limitations on tree growth and so on. *Land of the Snowshoe Hare* and other writings by Virginia S. Eifert (Dodd), describing the north woods of Wisconsin-Michigan, include interesting material on what she calls Canadian carpet plants: bunchberry, twinflower, and others.

Birdsbeak Pedicularis (Pedicularis ornithorhyncha)

Senecio (Senecio integerrimus), two views

These fluffy, tightly-packed flower heads waving in the wind are abundant in subalpine meadows. Mountain dock is a name long familiar to Northwest mountain hikers. The plant is also called American bistort and is an important component of alpine meadows in the Rockies. The adjective serves to distinguish this species from *Polygonum bistorta,* which grows both in European mountain meadows and two-thirds of the way around the world in the far north, to Alaska. Except that its flower is pink, the latter bistort is similar; this explains why ours was named *P. bistortoides,* meaning "bistort-like."

Mountain dock does not look very similar to its relatives, the wild buckwheats *(Eriogonums),* nor to rhubarb, but the leaves and stem will remind one of some of the weedy members of the family in genera *Rumex* and *Polygonum* (docks, smartweeds, knotweeds). Rhizomes are short, thick, and starchy, and eaten by small rodents. It has been discovered that the stem grows very quickly, sometimes about 4 inches or one-third of its height in a week. Because the floral envelope remains around the developing seed, the flower appears to last a long time and will be seen late in summer, though it is not as pretty and fluffy after the stamens are gone.

White bistort is another possible distinguishing name.

Photographed in late July at White Pass near Glacier Peak, with 35mm Canon camera on High Speed Ektachrome film.

Senecio

Senecios, sometimes called butterweeds, ragworts, or groundsels, are yellow "daisies" with yellow centers. The plants come in a variety of shapes and sizes, and they may be adapted to moderately-dry, well-drained soils as is this species, to scree slopes, or to boggy or streamside habitats. Often the flowers are rather ragged looking because of short and scattered rays. Senecios can be told from the similar arnicas, also found in the Cascades in a number of species, by the fact that their leaves always alternate up the stem. First on one side, then on another. Leaves of the arnicas appear in pairs, opposite each other on the stem.

Senecio integerrimus is a species of the Great Plains, with a range from valleys to timberline, from Saskatchewan to British Columbia, to Colorado and California. This is an amazing enough range, even though botanists recognize several varieties. It is not surprising, then, that it is found mainly on the east side of the Cascades. The short, thickened flower head in the center is typical; also note that the leaves are gradually reduced in size up the stem. It is usually about a foot tall, more or less, and grows on grassy slopes.

The arrowhead senecio, *S. triangularis,* may be identified by a leafy stem and the arrow-shaped leaves remaining about the same size all the way to the top. Also widespread, it is the species most common on the west side — late-blooming, growing by streams or in moist hollows of subalpine meadows, about 2 feet high.

Over a thousand species of senecio are recognized, making it one of the largest genera of flowering plants. Some, on high mountains in the African and South American tropics, are giants, becoming almost like small trees, with unusual silhouettes. The florist's cineraria, whose dark red and purple shades contrast so strongly with white markings, is another senecio, one which came originally from the Canary Islands. Ours are mostly yellow, occasionally with a slight orange tinge, or a variation toward a cream color. Make the second "e" long, and accent it.

Two views of a particularly pretty specimen of Senecio integerrimus, taken on Desolation Peak above Ross Lake, with a 35mm Canon camera on High Speed Ektachrome film. This senecio may also be found on Miners Ridge.

179

Alpine Aster (Aster alpigenus)

Below and right, Aster (Aster species)

Alpine Aster

A dwarf, alpine aster with more intense color than its taller relatives, and just one blossom head on each stem. Most of the long, narrow leaves are basal. It grows at alpine and upper subalpine levels, on grassy or rocky slopes where vegetation is not dense, most abundantly on volcanic peaks such as Mount Rainier and Glacier Peak.

It ranges in the mountains from Washington to California, eastward to the Rockies. This is our "alpine aster"; there is another, more northern circumboreal alpine plant, *A. alpinus*, which has the same common name.

Alpine aster photographed on the Frozen Lake trail near Sunrise, Yakima Park, Mount Rainier, in mid-July, with 35mm Canon camera on High Speed Ektachrome film.

Aster

Aster species (Composite Family)

More ubiquitous are the familiar, tall-stemmed asters with several or many flower heads. Several similar-looking species are common, and some may be seen on almost any late summer or early fall drive or hike.

A high-angle closeup view of the same tall aster pictured on the opposite page. Taken on the Naches Peak trail near Chinook Pass, with 35mm Canon camera on High Speed Ektachrome film.

Aster

The best way to tell asters from daisies is to let the experts identify them for you. At lower elevations a general rule is that *Erigerons* bloom in spring and early summer while asters bloom in late summer and fall. In the mountains where the growing season is shorter, their blooming times tend to merge. Though there are other *Erigerons* with many heads on a stem, in the Washington Cascades mountain daisy (*E. peregrinus*) can quickly be eliminated by its single heads; stems with many heads are those of asters. (Notice that this cannot be phrased in the opposite way, as the alpine aster also has but one blossom head.) Comparing the pictures and forming a visual memory of their appearance will help; the daisy has a flatter look and the aster is uplifted. Bracts under the aster flower head grow in several rows, imbricated like shingles on a roof; in *Erigeron* they are mostly in the same plane. In most cases *Erigerons* have more rays and asters have a leafier stem.

Tall asters (one to 2 or 3 feet) common in various situations in the Cascades include *A. ledophyllus, A. foliaceus, A. modestus,* and *A. engelmanni.* Color varies from pink-purple to blue. Leaf and bract characteristics are important in distinguishing species; to the casual eye all are much alike.

Photograph made on the Naches Peak trail near Chinook Pass, with 35mm Canon camera on High Speed Ektachrome film.

Marmot

Below, Huckleberry in blossom. Right, Huckleberry in fruit (Vaccinium deliciosum)

Marmot

The marmot's interest in meadow flowers is gustatory rather than aesthetic. For about 4 months each year he eats subalpine vegetation, and the other 8 months he spends in hibernation.

Photographed while sunning on a rock beside his burrow (or doing sentry duty), in Edith Creek basin, Mount Rainier, using 200mm lens on 35mm Canon camera and High Speed Ektachrome film.

Huckleberry; Blueberry   *Vaccinium deliciosum* (Heath Family)

Huckleberries are to be eaten. Some require bending low, some are tall bushes, and some are in between; their flavors vary, too. Leaves as well as berries are utilized by wildlife. A favorite food of bears, they are also eaten by many other mammals, large and small, and by birds. As an extra dividend, several kinds form a very important part of the autumn color in the Cascades.

Naming each species is apt to prove frustrating. One can be recognized because the blossoms appear before the leaves; by the time the plant is in fruit, who's to know? Most keys rely on combinations of several characteristics which need to be checked out with care. In the pictures, note the fat blossoms, growing singly from the season's new growth, and the brown, roundish older branches. Note the shape of the leaves which

taper narrowly toward the attached end, and their paler (glaucous) color on the underside. Also, the large berry and its crowning ring which was formed by the calyx tube from which the rounded lobes have dropped off (some species retain their calyx lobes which can then be seen on the blossom end of the ripened berry, as in the red huckleberry pictured on p. 56).

First recognized as a new species on Mount Rainier in 1901, this low-growing huckleberry, *Vaccinium deliciosum*, grows only in the Olympics and the Cascades from southern British Columbia to northern Oregon and carpets mountain meadows with red in the fall. It badly needs a short common name of its own. The names alpine, mountain, dwarf, and lowbush are in use for other species; in any case these terms would apply equally well to others found in the Cascades. Several others are just as characteristic of the Northwest. Of the eight or nine kinds we have, at least four others are blue. It has been called delicious huckleberry, a translation of the specific name, but the verdict of generations of berry tasters is not with early Washington botanist Charles Piper who named it; instead the black huckleberry has their vote as the most delicious. Many might call it next best. It is sweet, with a taste just

Huckleberry blossoms photographed on Round Mountain near Darrington, with 35mm Canon camera on Kodachrome II film.

186

faintly reminiscent of bananas; a handful is the perfect complement to make instant banana pudding a mountain epicure's delight.

The blueness of some kinds is an illusion, the result of a pale bloom which can be rubbed off and which disappears in cooking—whether "blue" or "black," both come out a deep purple and both stain fingers and lips with the same shade. Several blues are sweet as this one is; others are somewhat acid. The black huckleberry, *Vaccinium membranaceum*, our only mountain huckleberry with black-appearing fruit, has a sweet and tangy flavor and is a great favorite wherever it grows. Besides the Cascades and Olympics, it is also to be found in the northern Rockies, usually growing 3 or 4 feet tall, but sometimes shorter, and providing clumps of bright color in fall.

Which ones are huckleberries and which ones are blueberries? The commercially-grown blueberry is also a *Vaccinium*, but a different species from any of our Northwest natives. The so-named huckleberries of eastern United States belong to a closely related genus in the heath family, the large-seeded *Gaylussacias*; the most well-known has black fruit.

Early European colonists in America found a great many new *Vacciniums*. Only four members of the clan were native to northern Europe: a small cranberry, the lingonberry favored by the Swedish for preserves to eat with pancakes, and two blue-berried plants called bilberries or whortleberries in England. Though separate names for each new American species were impossible, several of them had delectable sweet blue berries, and it became conventional to call them blueberries. For the new genus *Gaylussacia* was reserved a name derived from the English whortleberry, but now pronounced huckleberry. Blueberries were best eating.

Huckleberries that are huckleberries to easterners do not grow in the Northwest. We have only *Vacciniums*—blueberries—except that they are as apt to have red or black berries as blue ones. As a group, western *Vacciniums* differ from eastern blueberries in a variety of technical ways, the most obvious of which is a tendency to produce flowers and berries singly, somewhat hidden under the leaves, rather than in a large terminal cluster. With sure tribal instinct, folk speech returned to the use of the name huckleberry, related to the old whortleberry used in England for *Vacciniums*, but no longer a part of common American speech. As used in the Northwest, the term has no negative undertones; blueberries simply come from a berry farm by way of the supermarket, huckleberries are picked off a bush. It is permissable, though not necessary, to call the wild blue ones blueberries.

Ripe huckleberries photographed in late September on Tolmie Peak, Mount Rainier National Park, with 4x5-inch Super Graphic. Famous berrying spots include Mount Dickerman off the Mountain Loop Highway, the Mount Baker ski area, and hills west of Mount Adams.

Dwarf Fireweed (Epilobium latifolium)

Gentian (Gentiana calycosa), two views

Dwarf Fireweed

Like the common fireweed, another *Epilobium*, this is a pioneer. It does its pioneering on glacial till and on gravel river flats in the far North. In Iceland it is known by a name that translates into British English as shingle rose; in American this means gravel flat rose, appropriately descriptive, though not a pretty name in our language. Alaskans have come up with river beauty.

Dwarf fireweed is more common in the North Cascades than at Mount Rainier, the upper basins in the Stehekin valley and Price Lake under Mount Shuksan being two well-known sites for it. It blooms fairly late in the summer, on a short stem measured in inches rather than feet, with large flowers massed in a compact cluster. Gray green leaves are short and broad compared with those of the common fireweed; the species name "latifolium" means broad-leaved. *Epilobiums* are also called willow herbs because of the shape of the leaves (never mind that most of our Northwest willow leaves are not shaped that way). This one and the very tiny *Epilobium alpinum* that grows by cold alpine streams with the yellow monkeyflower often get the willow herb designation since they have nothing to do with fire.

Fireweeds (and evening primroses for that matter, but you will not find those in the Cascades), have an inferior ovary. Between the flower and the main stem is only a short flowerstalk; the rest is a long, narrow ovary that will develop into the seed case, a helpful point to check when trying to identify small four-petaled flowers. Members of the mustard family grow their seed capsules on the top side of the flower.

Sometimes this one and the common fireweed are separated from the other *Epilobiums* into another genus, *Chamaenerion*.

Photograph made in the Napeequa valley, Glacier Peak Wilderness Area, with 35mm Canon camera on High Speed Ektachrome.

190

Gentian

Gentian blooms at the end of the mountain flower season. With it, in September, may be seen a few last blossoms on arnicas, mountain dock, thistle, aster, bluebells. Sometimes flowers such as Tolmie saxifrage, or patches of lupine, bloom late in a certain spot because of long-lying snowbanks. Gentian, surrounded by browning plants already in seed, is late because it takes a long growing period. Development from bud into flower is slow; you can spot the gentian buds weeks before you see blossoms.

It is no surprise, considering the lengthy growth period, that gentian grows in moist soil (though there is an ecological variant that grows in drier places). It is found from British Columbia to California, east to the Rockies. Dr. William Tolmie, Hudson's Bay Company officer temporarily stationed at Fort Nisqually, collected the first specimen. An avid collector, he made an excursion to the north side of Mount Rainier, via the Puyallup and Mowich valleys, in 1833, with some Indian guides. The trip being feasible in late summer because of the availability of berries and game at this season, it was September 2 when Tolmie reached the top of Hessong Rock. In the vicinity of this peak he found a number of new flowers, including besides this gentian, alpine aster, Tolmie saxifrage, birdsbeak and coiled-beak pedicularis, fanleaf cinquefoil (*Potentilla flabellifolia*), and Tolmie penstemon.

Gentian will close in rainy weather, perhaps a protective device to prevent the flower cup filling with water. Plants average around 6 inches tall, flowers about an inch long. At moderate elevations on the dry east side it is found by watercourses; where there is more rain it grows in moist meadows.

(Top) Gentian photographed in mid-August beside Clover Lake, north of Sunrise Point, Mount Rainier National Park, with 35mm Canon camera on High Speed Ektachrome film.

(Bottom) Photographed in Glacier Basin, Mount Rainier; same camera and film.

191

Luetkea (Luetkea pectinata)

Tolmie Saxifrage (Saxifraga tolmiei)

Sedum or Stonecrop (Sedum divergens)

A miniature shrub which may form large mats in subalpine and alpine zones, the soft, feathery leaves studded with cream-colored blossom heads. A subshrub in technical language, only 3 or 4 inches tall, it would not strike most people as a shrub at all, but does have trailing woody stems. Often found where snow lasts late, and if the hiker comes upon a patch with leaves flat upon the ground, this means not that someone has been lying there, rather that the snow has just melted off. Tolmie saxifrage may be seen growing near it. However, the two are not usually intermingled.

A common characteristic is the adaptation to late-snow areas; seeing luetkea form a mat on the upper side of a big boulder and the saxifrage across its lower end in an otherwise bare, loose sandy slope suggests possible different moisture requirements and a need of a cooler root environment for the saxifrage. Study might bring out other factors involved.

Luetkea was named by a St. Petersburg botanist, August Bongard, in honor of Count Friedrich Leutke, active in that city's Academy of Sciences and commander of a Russian ship charting the Alaska coast in 1827. The plant was collected at Sitka by Carl Mertens. The other part of its name, "pectinata," means comb-like, doubtless in reference to its leaves with their long teeth. The leaves also account for a popular name, partridge foot, somewhat of a misnomer since it is grouse and ptarmigan that have feathered legs, not partridges; this name dates from days when hunters used the terms "grouse" and "partridge" interchangeably. Because it was for a while considered a species of spirea, it has been called Alaska spirea—not very appropriately, as it is more typical of Northwest mountains than of Alaska in general. Occasionally, also, alpine spirea.

Photographed on Mount David near Lake Wenatchee with 35mm Canon camera on High Speed Ektachrome film, in late August. Luetkea compares in size with the flowers on the opposite page; it is shown somewhat enlarged.

Tolmie Saxifrage

Saxifraga tolmiei (Saxifrage Family)

An alpine pioneer found where snow lies late, usually in rather sandy soil, often growing by a boulder or below a snowpatch, sometimes seen in a temporary snowmelt pool. Always alone—it is not a good competitor. Succulent leaves remind one of a sedum, but the paired seedpods are those of the saxifrages. Many kinds of saxifrages grow in the mountains beside shady streams, in cliff crevices, on dry trailbanks. Most have five small white petals, but can easily be told from small white flowers in the pink, purslane, or rose families by the unique ovaries with spreading beak, two together in a superior position. Leaves are all shapes and sizes, as varied as the habitats.

Tolmie saxifrage was named after its discoverer, William Fraser Tolmie, a medical officer of the Hudson's Bay Company, who made the first botanical collecting trip to Mount Rainier.

Photograph taken in late July shows it growing beneath a rock on White Mountain near Glacier Peak. 35mm Canon camera and High Speed Ektachrome film.

Sedum; Stonecrop

Sedum divergens (Stonecrop Family)

Waxed and succulent leaves store water to help the plant survive periods between rains on rocky outcrops with no seepage, and on other dry habitats where it grows. This is a subalpine and alpine species which may even be found on moraines beside glaciers. Distinguishing features, in addition to the almost globose shape of leaf, are that its five follicles (seedpods) spread outward (are divergent) and leaves on the flowering stem are opposite. Other yellow-flowered sedums, or stonecrops, commonly seen are *S. lanceolatum* with narrow leaves; and at lower elevations, *S. oreganum* with more flat, round leaves growing alternately on the stem, and erect follicles.

Sedum photographed in early July above Moraine Park, alongside the Carbon Glaicer on Mount Rainier. Taken with 4x5-inch Super Graphic. Reddish leaves are quite typical of this species at blooming time.

Grass

Red leaves are one statement of fall—huckleberries splashing color across an open slope, vine maple on rockslides. Golden heads of grass are another. Grasses are generally mixed in with the larger flowers, particularly on south-facing meadows, and they become more conspicuous after the broader-leaved plants have withered. Grass seeds are eaten by many birds and small mammals.

Wet meadows covered with sedge (recognized by its triangular stems) are also common in the mountains. Their foliage is important wildlife food. Not as many colorful flowers grow in these meadows, but the sedge plants (*Carex* species) have interesting patterns of flowering heads and seeds. So also have the woodrushes (*Luzula* species) which grow around clumps of trees.

Some kinds of grasses and sedges are usually included among the highest-growing alpine flowering plants. There are alpine species of bluegrass, timothy, fescue, bent grass, and others in less familiar genera; at higher levels they are not likely to form sods.

Grass turning brown in September on Bastile Ridge above Mount Baker's Coleman Glacier; taken with 35mm Canon camera on Kodachrome II film.

Golden Fleabane   *Erigeron aureus* (Composite Family)

This is an alpine plant, usually found on high ridges above timberline. The flora of rocky ridges, of cliff crevices and ledges differs from that of gently-sloping meadows which may be only a few feet below. Plants have to cope with problems of less soil and moisture and greater exposure to wind. The golden fleabane has some colorful companions here. One is the miniature ground-hugging Lyall lupine with balls of dark blue flowers instead of tall spikes, and fuzzy grayish leaves that form a mat. (It used to be known as *Lupinus lyallii*, but lately botanists have tossed it into the less distinctive *L. lepidus* var. *lobbii*.) With them also, may be found the flaming scarlet paintbrush, *Castilleja rupicola*, low in stature, with long flowers and purple leaves. Lichen-covered rocks add to the picture.

The golden fleabane is about 4 or 5 inches tall. With the lupine and the paintbrush it forms an alpine garden unique to the Washington Cascades, since the lupine alone extends much farther south, the paintbrush just a little. And neither of these last two grows east to the Canadian Rockies, as does the fleabane.

Besides the larger lavender fleabane (mountain daisy) of subalpine meadows, golden fleabane has several inconspicuous, pale-colored alpine relatives, and many others at lower elevations.

(Back cover) Golden fleabane growing between rocks near Frozen Lake above Sunrise in Yakima Park, Mount Rainier. Taken with 35mm Canon camera on High Speed Ektachrome film.

Wild Buckwheat *Eriogonum flavum* (Buckwheat Family)

Wild buckwheat, or eriogonum if you prefer (accent is on the "og"; vowels are short), is a genus fairly easy to recognize, but the various species are something more difficult. A sulphur-yellow shade, unique among our flowers, is found both in *Eriogonum flavum* and in *E. umbellatum.* Two taller white ones are *E. compositum* and *E. heracloides,* but the first sometimes comes in yellow, too, while *E. umbellatum* includes some varieties that are white, so you cannot depend on color. Each species has a different leaf and growth pattern, but there are variations which come close to one of the others; eventually you look for such details as hair on the back of the individual flowers, which helps to distinguish *E. flavum* from others which might look like it. Flowers are arranged in umbels, often flat-topped, sometimes ball-shaped; the cushion eriogonum, *E. ovalifolium,* forms a cushion of gray felted leaves decorated with balls of creamy flowers that often turn pink with age. Another dwarf, found at high altitudes, is the very inconspicuous *E. pyrolaefolium.* Reddish buds are sometimes seen in any of the eriogonums, and a pinkish tinge is very common as the blossoms age—they become papery and remain on the plant a long time.

The buckwheat of pancakes is distantly related; so is the bistort, or mountain dock. Eriogonums are plants of the arid West; predictably, we find them more common on the east side of the Cascades. The plant pictured is growing on a high sunny, west-facing ridge slope. Below it is a typical U-shaped glaciated valley.

Photographed on Little Giant Pass above Napeequa valley in the Glacier Peak Wilderness Area, in mid-August, with 35mm Canon camera on High Speed Ektachrome film.

FAMILIES REPRESENTED IN THIS BOOK ARE:

FERN FAMILY
Oak Fern, Gymnocarpium dryopteris, 18

GRASS FAMILY
Grass, 198

ARUM FAMILY
Skunk Cabbage, Lysichitum americanum, 11

LILY FAMILY
Clintonia, Clintonia uniflora, 43
Glacier Lily, Erythronium grandiflorum, 90, 91
Avalanche Lily, Erythronium montanum, 95, 98
Columbia Tiger Lily, Lilium columbianum, 111
False Solomon's Seal, Smilacina racemosa, 71
Rosy Twisted Stalk, Streptopus roseus, 66
Trillium, Trillium ovatum, 14, 15
White Hellebore, Veratrum californicum, 123
Green Hellebore, Veratrum viride, 122
Beargrass, Xerophyllum tenax, 166

ORCHID FAMILY
Calypso, Calypso bulbosa, 34
Coralroot, Corallorhiza mertensiana, 38, 39
White Bog Orchid, Habenaria dilatata, 86

BIRTHWORT FAMILY
Wild Ginger, Asarum caudatum, 35

BUCKWHEAT FAMILY
Wild Buckwheat, Eriogonum sp., 201
Bistort, Polygonum bistortoides, 178

PURSLANE FAMILY
Spring Beauty, Claytonia lanceolata, 103
Columbia Lewisia, Lewisia columbiana, 170
Tweedy's Lewisia, Lewisia tweedyi, 170

BUTTERCUP FAMILY
Western Anemone, Anemone occidentalis, 102, 103
Columbine, Aquilegia formosa, 127
Marsh Marigold, Caltha biflora, 87
Buttercup, Ranunculus eschscholtzii, 94

BARBERRY FAMILY
Vanilla Leaf, Achlys triphylla, 27

FUMITORY FAMILY
Corydalis, Corydalis scouleri, 46, 47
Bleeding Heart, Dicentra formosa, 30

STONECROP FAMILY
Stonecrop, Sedum divergens, 195

SAXIFRAGE FAMILY
Tolmie Saxifrage, Saxifraga tolmiei, 195
Foamflower, Tiarella unifoliata, 26

ROSE FAMILY
Luetkea, Luetkea pectinata, 194
Creeping Raspberry, Rubus lasiococcus, 74
Salmonberry, Rubus spectabilis, 78
Mountain Ash, Sorbus scopulina, 151
Rosy Spirea, Spirea densiflora, 130

PEA FAMILY
Lupine, Lupinus latifolia, 143

BUCKTHORN FAMILY
Snowbrush, Ceanothus velutinous, 83

VIOLET FAMILY
Blue Violet, Viola adunca, 107
Tall Yellow Violet, Viola glabella, 31
Marsh Violet, Viola palustris, 78

EVENING PRIMROSE FAMILY
Fireweed, Epilobium angustifolium, 75
Dwarf Fireweed, Epilobium latifolium, 190

GINSENG FAMILY
Devil's Club, Oplopanax horridum, 23

PARSLEY FAMILY
Cow Parsnip, Heracleum lanatum, 110
Meadow Parsley, Ligusticum grayi, 126
Lomatum, Lomatium sp., 107

DOGWOOD FAMILY
Canadian Dogwood, Cornus canadensis, 50, 51

HEATH FAMILY
White Heather, Cassiope mertensiana, 118
Pipsissewa, Chimaphila unbellata, 67
Salal, Gaultheria shallon, 58
Pinesap, Hypopitys monotropa, 63
Menziesia, Menziesia ferruginea, 59
Indian Pipe, Monotropa uniflora, 62
Red Heather, Phyllodoce empetriformis, 119
Pink Pyrola, Pyrola asarifolia, 54
Sidebells Pyrola, Pyrola secunda, 55
Woodnymph, Pyrola uniflora, 66
White Rhododendron, Rhododendron albiflorum, 131
Huckleberry, Vaccinium deliciosum, 186, 187
Red Huckleberry, Vaccinium parvifolium, 58

PRIMROSE FAMILY
Shooting Star, Dodecatheon jeffreyi, 79

GENTIAN FAMILY
Gentian, Gentiana calycosa, 191

PHLOX FAMILY
Scarlet Gilia, Gilia aggregata, 82
Phlox, Phlox diffusa, 106
Jacob's Ladder, Polemonium pulcherrimum, 142

BORAGE FAMILY
Mertensia, Mertensia paniculata, 70

FIGWORT FAMILY
Magenta Paintbrush, Castilleja parviflora, 135, 139
White Paintbrush, Castilleja parviflora, 138
Monkeyflower, Mimulus sp., 158
Pink Monkeyflower, Mimulus lewisii, 162, 163
Alpine Monkeyflower, Mimulus tilingii, 159
Elephanthead, Pedicularis groenlandica, 171
Birdsbeak Pedicularis, Pedicularis ornithorhyncha, 174
Rainier Pedicularis, Pedicularis rainierensis, 175

BLADDERWORT FAMILY
Butterwort, Pinguicula vulgaris, 155

HONEYSUCKLE FAMILY
Twinflower, Linnaea borealis, 42

BLUEBELL FAMILY
Bluebell, Campanula rotundifolia, 150

COMPOSITE FAMILY
Pussytoes, Antennaria sp., 167
Arnica, Arnica latifolia, 151
Aster, Aster sp., 183
Alpine Aster, Aster alpigenus, 182
Thistle, Cirsium edule, 154
Golden Fleabane, Erigeron aureus, 199
Mountain Daisy, Erigeron peregrinus, 146
Coltsfoot, Petasites frigidus, 22
Senecio, Senecio integerrimus, 179

INDEX

OTHER BOOKS FROM THE MOUNTAINEERS

THE HIKES SERIES

100 Hikes in Western Washington

Hikes ranging in variety from ocean beach to mountain peak, in length from short days to full weeks. Text by Louise B. Marshall, photos by Bob and Ira Spring, maps by Marge Mueller.

101 Hikes in the North Cascades

A selection from the best hikes, short and long, in the North Cascades National Park, Ross Lake and Lake Chelan National Recreation Areas, Glacier Peak and Pasayten Wilderness Areas, and surrounding lands. Text by Ira Spring and Harvey Manning, photos by Bob and Ira Spring, maps by Helen Sherman. To be published in Summer 1970.

102 Hikes in the Alpines Lakes and South Cascades and the Olympics

To be published in Summer 1971.

50 Hikes in Mount Rainier National Park

Descriptions of every trail in the park. Some of the most popular as well as some of the lonesomest trails in the West. Text by Ira Spring and Harvey Manning, photos by Bob and Ira Spring, maps by Marge Mueller. Published jointly with the Mount Rainier Natural History Association.

Trips and Trails, 1: Family Camps, Short Hikes, and View Roads in the North Cascades and Olympics

Places to camp, short trails to walk, things to see and do — mountain and beach recreation for the whole family. Text by E. M. Sterling, photos by Bob and Ira Spring, maps by Marge Mueller.

Trips and Trails, 2: Family Camps, Short Hikes, and View Roads in Mount Rainier and the South Cascades

Companion volume to the above. Features a coding to separate the easier hikes from the more difficult, the smooth roads from the bumpier.

Northwest Ski Trails

A guide to the best area skiing and ski touring in Washington, Oregon, and British Columbia. Includes a 20-page section on equipment, techniques, and hazards peculiar to ski touring. Text by Ted Mueller, photos by Bob and Ira Spring, maps by Marge Mueller.

Footloose around Puget Sound: 100 Walks on Beaches, Lowlands, and Foothills

Pleasant strolls along beaches, easy trails, abandoned or seldom-used country roads, and through city and state parks. Text by Janice Krenmayr, photos by Bob and Ira Spring, maps by Helen Sherman.

OTHER GUIDES

Routes and Rocks: Hiker's Guide to the North Cascades from Glacier Peak to Lake Chelan

Trails and off-trail high routes in and around the the Glacier Peak Wilderness Area, with notes on geology. 96 drawings and maps, 8 photos, 3 quadrangle maps in back pocket. By D. F. Crowder and R. W. Tabor.

Hiker's Map to the North Cascades: Routes and Rocks in the Mt. Challenger Quadrangle

Also by Crowder and Tabor, covering the Picket Range and Custer Ridge.

Trail Country: Olympic National Park

Mile-by-mile guide to every trail in the park, with chapters on natural and human history. 25 photographs, 25 maps. By Robert L. Wood.

Guide to Leavenworth Rock Climbing Areas

Complete descriptions of routes, difficult moves, hardware used, etc. 10 sketches, 2 sketch maps. By Fred Beckey and Eric Bjornstad.

Snowshoe Hikes in the Cascades and Olympics

Easy walks for the beginner, strenuous ascents for the winter mountaineer. More than 80 trips, each with sketch map. 13 photos. By Gene Prater.

TECHNIQUE

Mountaineering: The Freedom of the Hills

Textbook of the Climbing Course. Chapters on every aspect of climbing, hiking, camping. 140 drawings, 16 photos. Edited by Harvey Manning.

Medicine for Mountaineering

A complete doctor book prepared by climber-physicians with experience from the Himalaya to the Cascades. Edited by James A. Wilkerson.

Mountaineering First Aid

First-aid-kit size pamphlet, reprinting the chapter from **Freedom of the Hills.**

Mountain Rescue Techniques

Published in cooperation with the Oesterreichi-scher Alpenverein and Mountain Rescue Council. The official manual of the International Commission for Alpine Rescue. By Wastl Mariner.

GENERAL

The North Cascades

68 high-mountain photographs from a climber's viewpoint. Displayed on 10x12-inch pages. By Tom Miller.

Across the Olympic Mountains: The Press Expedition, 1889-90

Detailed story of a classic wilderness exploration. Published jointly with the University of Washington Press. By Robert L. Wood.

Challenge of the North Cascades

Stirring narratives of the author's first ascents over a 30-year period, by Fred Beckey. 12 maps, 48 photographs.

Challenge of Mount Rainier

By Dee Molenaar. The first 100 years of climbing on The Mountain, with narratives of ascents and detailed descriptions of all routes. Many photos, drawings, and maps. Due 1970.

The Mountaineers

Information about the history of the club, its activities, and how to join.

For a descriptive catalogue of these books and others in production, write Mountaineer Books, P.O. Box 122, Seattle, Washington 98111.